D0784533

TRAVELLERS

NAMIBIA

By
SUE DOBSON

Thomas Cook

Written by Sue Dobson
Original photography by Sue Dobson

Published by Thomas Cook Publishing
A division of Thomas Cook Tour Operations Limited
Company registration no 1450464 England
The Thomas Cook Business Park, 9 Coningsby Road,
Peterborough PE3 8SB, United Kingdom
Email: books@thomascook.com, Tel: + 44 (0) 1733 416477
www.thomascookpublishing.com

Produced by Cambridge Publishing Management Limited
Burr Elm Court, Main Street, Caldecote CB23 7NU

ISBN: 978-1-84157-947-4

© 2008 Thomas Cook Publishing
Text © Thomas Cook Publishing
Maps © Thomas Cook Publishing/PCGraphics (UK) Limited

Series Editor: Linda Bass
Production/DTP: Steven Collins

Printed and bound in Italy by Printer Trento

Cover photography: Front L–R: © Chris Simpson/Getty Images; © Pavan
Aldo/SIME-4Corners Images; © Fantuz Olimpio/SIME-4Corners Images
Back L–R: © Fantuz Olimpio/SIME-4Corners Images; © Fantuz Olimpio/
SIME-4Corners Images

The paper used for this book has been independently certified as having
been sourced from well-managed forests and recycled wood or fibre
according to the rules of the Forest Stewardship Council.
This book has been printed and bound in Italy by Printer Trento S.r.l.,
an FSC certified company for printing books on FSC mixed paper in
compliance with the chain of custody and on products labelling standards.

FSC
Mixed Sources
Product group from well-managed
forests and recycled wood or fibre
Cert no. CQ-COC-000012
www.fsc.org
© 1996 Forest Stewardship Council

Contents

Introduction

An estimated 2.1 million people occupy 824,268sq km (318,252sq miles) of land, 60 per cent of which is desert or semi-desert, making Namibia one of the most sparsely populated nations on earth. They belong to a dozen different ethnic groups, speak 25 different languages or major dialects and live in a landscape as old as time where conservation matters so much it is enshrined in the constitution.

Namibia is a country of infinite space where herds of wild animals roam and birds soar into an impossibly blue sky. It is a pristine environment of sand and rock, bush and plain, steep cliffs, high mountains and vast open spaces. Here you'll find the world's oldest desert, Africa's answer to the Grand Canyon, and plants, birds, insects and animals found nowhere else on earth.

Desert-adapted elephants roam the dry riverbeds of the north. The strange *Welwitschia mirabilis* is the oldest plant known to man and lives for hundreds of years. Endangered black rhino roam free in Namibia, which is home to more cheetah than any other country.

Towering sand dunes in a 'sand sea' the size of Switzerland sweep inland from the coast, where diamonds are sucked from the seabed. Dinosaurs once roamed across the great escarpment and left their footprints for all to see. Six thousand years ago at Twyfelfontein, the San (Bushmen) inscribed rocks with so many images that the site has gained World Heritage status.

This is a land of hauntingly beautiful landscapes and vistas so grand you learn the true meaning of the word 'awesome'. It is also a land of welcoming people, where smiles are genuine and kindness comes as second nature.

Often perceived as an 'appendage' to South Africa – and for decades under Apartheid's cruel and divisive thumb – Namibia had a lot of catching up to do when independence finally came in 1990. After a long and bitter liberation struggle, which saw thousands of Namibians fleeing the country and living in exile, education was a priority for the new government, as was healing wounds and working towards a better understanding between black and white Namibians. Both have been successfully achieved.

Over the years, the country's infrastructure has been much improved and tourism is no longer a fledgling industry. Distances are long but getting around is made easy with well-maintained roads and numerous light aircraft charters. Some of the finest lodges in Africa offer superb accommodation and memorable food in take-your-breath-away locations. Countless campsites and rest camps, guesthouses, B&Bs and guest farms make travelling on a budget quite feasible.

For the seeker of adventure Namibia can offer sand boarding down dunes 130m (425ft) high with steep slip faces of soft, powder-like sand, quad biking, rock climbing, mountain biking, horse riding through canyons, hot-air ballooning, paragliding and some of the most challenging hiking in Africa.

For those who like quieter pursuits, there's excellent coastal fishing with big catches almost guaranteed and freshwater angling in well-stocked lakes and dams. Golfers will find an 18-hole, fully grassed desert course where springbok share the greens. Guided walks through unforgettable landscapes offer an introduction to the strange and wonderful world of ancient trees and intriguing plants traditionally used for medicines. For the wildlife enthusiast, Namibia is Eden.

More and more visitors are discovering not only that Namibia has so much to offer, but also how very different it is from its next-door neighbours. Scenically, Namibia may not be how most people imagine Africa to look, but therein lies its charm: it is different, surprising and endlessly fascinating.

The automobile is celebrated with a sense of humour at the Cañon Roadhouse, a lodge and restaurant near the Fish River Canyon

The land

Namibia is not how you expect Africa to be. Dominated by the Namib Desert and soaring dunes, its landscape spans vast open plains, hills and mountains, a barren coastline, strange rock formations and Africa's Grand Canyon. In this country of 824,268sq km (318,252sq miles) are rivers wide and fast flowing – and rivers that may spend years as dry sandy beds before suddenly, and briefly, turning into raging torrents.

Rivers form Namibia's frontiers with its neighbours, the Orange River with South Africa, and the Kunene and Okavango rivers with Angola in the north. The Kwando River not only marks Namibia's borders with Angola and Zambia but also, after it has flowed through the Caprivi Strip, with Botswana. The mighty Zambezi separates Namibia from Zambia before reaching the Victoria Falls in Zimbabwe. In between lies a landscape that changes from the lush green of the far north to dry parched wilderness and, the further south you go, vast desert.

Situated between South Africa and Angola on the bottom southwestern corner of Africa and straddling the Tropic of Capricorn, the country is about the size of France and the UK combined, or twice the size of California. A rugged escarpment separates a huge inland plateau from a narrow coastal plain washed by the South Atlantic Ocean. When the first Portuguese explorers set foot on the coast in the 15th century, they reported a place so barren it took another three centuries, and the 'Scramble for Africa' (see *p8*), before other Europeans started taking an interest in what the country might have to offer.

The coast

The desert meets the sea along an arid coastline stretching for 1,628km (1,012 miles). In the south it is inhabited at Oranjemund, a diamond-mining town closed to visitors, and at Lüderitz, which reveals its German ancestry in pastel-painted architecture. Around the deep natural harbour at Walvis Bay, the centre of Namibia's fishing industry, are some of Africa's most important coastal wetlands. Thousands of greater and lesser flamingos winter on the lagoon that feeds up to 200,000 shorebirds and migrating visitors.

The cold Benguela Current in the South Atlantic causes the coastal plain to be enveloped in a morning fog that delivers moisture to desert plants like

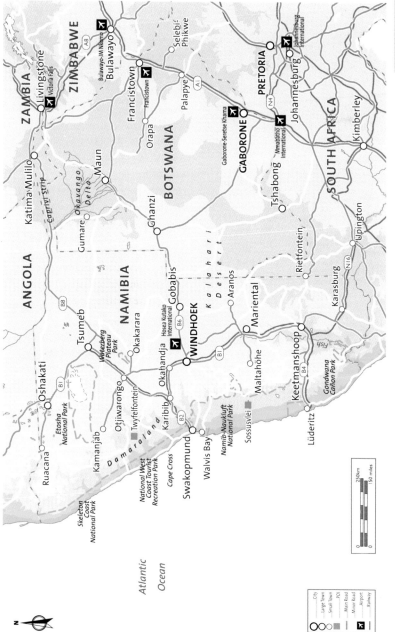

Desert-adapted elephants are a rare sight

the extraordinary *Welwitschia mirabilis* and the world's most extensive lichen fields. It makes swimming at Swakopmund, Namibia's summer playground, an exercise for the hardy, but the dunes that line the coastal road between the town and Walvis Bay are the setting for activities that give Swakopmund its reputation as an 'adventure capital'. Henties Bay, a holiday resort favoured by anglers, is the last coastal town. From there on, the bleak, windswept, mist-shrouded Skeleton Coast, with its shimmering saltpans and roaring dunes, is the territory of seal colonies and shipwrecks.

Inland to the east of the Skeleton Coast, the rock-strewn plains, hills and flat-topped mountains of rugged Kaokoland are home to desert-dwelling elephant, black rhino and giraffe, and the semi-nomadic Himba people. The much more accessible Damaraland tells of the ancient San people who left thousands of engravings on rocks, mountains and granite outcrops that glow red in the setting sun.

Plains and plateaux

A great silvery pan lies at the heart of the Etosha National Park, covering almost a quarter of the park's 22,912sq km (8,846sq miles) where over 100 animal species roam the mopane woodland, savannah, grassland and open plains that also provide a habitat for over 300 bird species. The pan is the remains of an inland lake, emptied millions of years ago. After good rains it holds shallow water for a few months, growing algae that attracts waterbirds by the thousand.

THE 'SCRAMBLE FOR AFRICA'

By the late 19th century, European powers, in particular Britain, France, Portugal and Belgium, had the vast resources of Africa in their sights for imperial expansion. In southern Africa, the British moved to annexe Walvis Bay for its harbour, later backing Germany's claim to South West Africa. Diamond magnate Cecil Rhodes, with his ambition of building a railway between the Cape Colony and Cairo, dreamed of Britain controlling the entire continent.

The race to take over Africa was fraught with rivalries. An international conference held in Berlin in 1884 began the carving up of Africa by the colonial powers. By 1902, 90 per cent of Africa was under European control.

In complete contrast, the very far north of the country is green and lush. It is the most populated area and the only region receiving enough rain for small-scale agriculture. The woodland and riverine vegetation of the Caprivi Strip supports much wildlife.

Namibia's best farming country occupies the high lands of the central plateau, among grassland and gently rolling hills. The capital, Windhoek, stands on the plateau, sheltered to the east and south by mountains. To the east, the land slopes off into the red desert sands of the Kalahari, which support some vegetation. Beyond the Khomas Hochland ('hilly highlands') to the west, the plateau falls away into a steep, dramatically incised escarpment and the great arid Namib Desert.

Desert and canyon

Between 80 and 140km (50 and 87 miles) wide, the Namib Desert, one of the world's oldest deserts, stretches the length of the Atlantic coastline and occupies about a fifth of Namibia's total area. It encompasses an impassable sea of towering dunes, rugged mountains and flat gravel plains that resemble a moonscape, and offers a home to desert-adapted animals and plants found nowhere else on earth.

The Fish River Canyon lies in the sparsely populated far south of the country. Stretching for 160km (100 miles), up to 27km (17 miles) wide and reaching a depth of 542m (1,778ft), it is one of Africa's great natural wonders.

A road bridge crosses a dry riverbed in the inhospitable Kuiseb Canyon

History

100,000 BC Archaeological evidence, including stone implements and ostrich eggshell beads, indicates that northern Namibia was inhabited during the Stone Age.

27,000 BC The oldest rock paintings date from this period. They are believed to be the work of the hunter-gatherer San people (Bushmen) who lived in small groups and roamed the land for food and water.

1st century AD The San are joined by the Khoikhoi (Nama) people, pastoralists migrating from the Botswana region and speaking a similar language based on click sounds.

c. 800 Quite where the Damara people came from is disputed, but they were settled in Namibia in the 9th century and spoke a Khoisan language.

1486 The first European to set foot in the country, Portuguese explorer Diogo Cão, erects a *padrão* (large stone pillar inscribed with the Portuguese coat of arms) at Cape Cross on the Skeleton Coast.

1488 Portuguese explorer Bartolomeu Dias lands on the coast at a place he names Terra de Santa Barbara, probably in the present-day Swakopmund area, and erects a *padrão* at a bay he names Angra de São Christóvão, today's Lüderitz.

c. 1550 The first Bantu-speaking people, the Herero, arrive from east Africa. Originally settling with their cattle in the north of the country, over the years they thrive and spread southwards.

1723–31 The Dutch West India Company sends whaling ships to Walvis Bay. By the late 18th century, American, British and French whalers are also using Walvis Bay and Lüderitz.

1793 Recognising the importance of the natural deep harbour, the Dutch authorities in the Cape of South Africa take possession of Walvis Bay.

Early 1800s Bands of Oorlam, Khoisan people dispossessed by the Dutch settlers of the Cape, cross the Orange River and settle among the southern Nama.

1805 The first missionaries, from London, arrive. They are soon followed by German Rhenish and Finnish Lutherans.

1840 An agreement between the Nama Chief Oaseb and the Oorlam leader Jonker Afrikaner brings the two groups closer together.

1851 British scientist Francis Galton and Swedish explorer Charles John Andersson are the first Europeans to reach the Etosha Pan.

1868 The Basters, Afrikaans-speaking mixed-race people from the Northern Cape, move into Namibia and settle around Rehoboth.

1878 Britain annexes Walvis Bay and incorporates it into the Cape Colony.

1884 The German flag is hoisted at Lüderitz Bay. The coastal zone between the rivers Oranje and Kunene is declared a 'protectorate', to be named German South West Africa.

1890s Indigenous people are systematically dispossessed of their land, which German settlers farm.

1893–4 Battles between the Witbooi Nama and German troops erupt when the Nama refuse to sign a 'protection' treaty.

1904–6 An uprising by the Herero and Nama people against maltreatment under colonial rule leads to death and destruction throughout the country and the setting up by the German military of concentration and forced-labour camps. General Lothar von Trotha issues his notorious 'Herero extermination' order.

1908 The first diamond is found near Lüderitz. The diamond rush is on.

1914–15 At the outbreak of World War I, the British-ruled Union of South Africa sends in battleships and troops. In July 1915,

German Schutztruppe (colonial troops) surrender at Khorab.

1920 The League of Nations gives South Africa the mandate to govern the territory of South West Africa.

1922 As white settlement is expanded and more land distributed to South African and German settlers, 'native reserves' are established for black Namibians.

1946 The United Nations, successor to the League of Nations, demands that South Africa hand back its mandate. South Africa refuses and seeks to annex the territory.

1948 Apartheid is officially instituted in South Africa and South West Africa.

1959 South African police ruthlessly crush resistance to the forced removal of Namibian people from Windhoek to Katutura Township.

1960 A national liberation group, the South West Africa People's Organisation (SWAPO), is formed,

under the leadership of Sam Nujoma in exile.

1966 The first clashes between South African troops and SWAPO launch the armed 'liberation war'. The United Nations terminates South Africa's mandate over South West Africa, but South Africa refuses to withdraw.

1968 The UN declares South Africa's occupation illegal and changes the country's name to Namibia.

1971 South Africa's presence in the country is ruled illegal by the International Court of Justice.

1973 The UN recognises SWAPO as the authentic representation of the people of Namibia.

1975 Neighbouring Angola becomes an independent nation and offers SWAPO bases near its southern border. South African troops invade Angola. Guerrilla warfare intensifies.

1977 South Africa declares the enclave of Walvis Bay to be part of the Cape Province.

1979–83 South Africa sets up an 'Internal Government' under racial lines in Namibia.

1989 Official ceasefire ends the long, bitterly fought bush war. Sam Nujoma returns after 30 years in exile, along with thousands of Namibians who had fled their country. Elections, overseen by UNTAG (United Nations Transition Assistance Group), are held in November.

1990 Independence. The Republic of Namibia is born on 21 March. Sam Nujoma is the first president. Namibia joins the United Nations. Walvis Bay, however, remains a South African enclave.

1991 State visit by HM Queen Elizabeth II after Namibia becomes a member of the Commonwealth.

1994 Walvis Bay, previously disputed by South Africa, is incorporated into Namibia. SWAPO is returned to power in a general election. The Namibian dollar, a new currency, is introduced.

It is linked to the South African rand.

2002 Land reform initiated on the principle of the sale and purchase of land by consent.

2004 Germany apologises to the Herero people for massacres perpetrated during its colonial rule, but will not consider compensation. Presidential elections in November result in a landslide victory for SWAPO's Hifikepunye Pohamba, a founder member of the party and chosen successor of former President Sam Nujoma.

2005 Mr Pohamba extends the programme of land reform.

2006 World coverage of the news that Angelina Jolie and Brad Pitt are travelling to Namibia for the birth of their baby results in an increase in tourism.

2007–8 Etosha Centenary Year celebrations highlight Namibia's conservation achievements with environmental projects, a new issue of postage stamps, art exhibitions and events.

Politics

After over a century of harsh colonial and apartheid rule, and a long, bitterly fought liberation war, Namibia's government has been working to improve life for the country's two million inhabitants. The country's constitution, adopted on independence in 1990, is recognised internationally as liberal and democratic. It guarantees fundamental human and civil rights, and a multi-party democracy governed by the rule of law.

When the long bush war ended and Sam Nujoma, legendary leader of the South West Africa People's Organisation (SWAPO), returned from exile in Zambia, there was no doubt that he and his party would rule newly independent Namibia. Indeed, in the country's first free and fair elections held in November 1989, SWAPO won decisively. But not unanimously. Six other political parties also gained seats in the Constituent Assembly, thus allaying fears of a one-party state. Between them, they agreed on a constitution that has been hailed as one of the most democratic in the world.

President Sam Nujoma and SWAPO were returned to power in the 1994 elections. The constitution allowed for only two terms of office for the elected president, so concerns were expressed when, in 1998, parliament passed an amendment allowing for a third term of office for Dr Nujoma. He stepped down in 2004, his chosen successor the 70-year-old Hifikepunye Pohamba, a fellow exile and founder member of SWAPO. Both he and the party won landslide victories in that year's elections, and President Pohamba was sworn in with due ceremony in March 2005.

Namibia has a strong system of regional and local government. Members of the National Council, the 'second house' in the country's bicameral parliament, are drawn from 13 Regional Councils elected every six years. General elections are held every five years for the 72-seat National Assembly. A system of proportional representation ensures the existence of minority parties.

Overcoming the past

While the new government inherited good infrastructure, it had the results of a painful past to contend with, particularly issues of land, poor education and health care, poverty, unemployment and a badly damaged economy.

Education, training and improving health-care facilities were high priorities, consuming a third of the country's budget. Mining, fishing and now tourism are the backbone industries and have seen investment and development. Immediately on independence, the government proclaimed Namibia's internationally recognised 200-nautical mile Exclusive Economic Zone which, together with strict marine conservation and management measures, has resulted in a successful fishing industry. Severe unemployment, however, continues to be a major problem.

Statistics can show that Namibia has one of the highest per-capita incomes in sub-Saharan Africa, but the income is distributed unevenly between white and black, urban and rural inhabitants. Although most Namibians now have access to electricity, running water and better living conditions, there is still much poverty.

At independence, 75 per cent of the population lived on 43 per cent of the land, with white farmers owning much of Namibia's best farmland. Land reform and redistribution began under President Nujoma, on the basis of mutual agreement between seller and buyer.

Namibia is the first country in the world to include protection of the environment in its constitution. About 15 per cent of the land is designated as national park. Linking conservation with community development, the government's conservation policy has proved a success story. By preserving the wildlife and environment in their area, local communities are benefiting financially from tourism, and the number of community-run projects such as campsites and guiding is growing.

Surrounded by gardens, Namibia's elegant Parliament building in Windhoek was formerly known as the Tintenpalast (Ink Palace)

Culture

From the early rock paintings and ritual dancing of the Bushmen to today's vibrant art and sounds of the townships, the peoples of Namibia have long revealed their lives through art and music. Throughout the colonial and apartheid eras, European artforms dominated, but independence has brought a flowering of traditional arts, crafts and music and a blending of African and Western cultures that is creating a sense of nationhood.

Art

Ranging in age from around 4,000 to 27,000 years, the countless rock paintings and engravings to be seen around Twyfelfontein and Brandberg in Damaraland and in the south of Namibia represent some of the world's oldest art.

They are believed to be the work of the early nomadic, hunter-gatherer San (Bushmen) people who painted animals, human figures and abstract images on flat rock, in caves and on overhangs, in monochrome red or in a mix of colours depending on the local geology. They also incised thousands of images on rocks and boulders.

Many experts believe they were connected with shamanic rituals. Sites hidden between large boulders indicate that they could have been ceremonial places, while engravings and paintings of giraffe in scenes incorporating clouds and rainbows suggest the giraffe was considered an animal with the power to bring rain.

In the colonial and apartheid years of the 19th and 20th centuries, most art seen in Namibia was by and for Europeans. Neighbouring South Africa, where the term 'township art' was coined, was a major influence in the development of aspiring black artists, especially from the 1960s onwards.

The first black Namibian artist to gain international acclaim was John Muafangejo. His distinctive black-and-white linocut images of biblical scenes and depictions of daily life and the liberation struggle are now widely sought after. An Owambo from northern Namibia, he died in 1987 at the age of just 44. He has influenced a contemporary generation of printmakers and given his name to an art school in Windhoek that specialises in print making, painting and sculpture.

Many private art galleries, particularly in Windhoek and Swakopmund, exhibit works by current Namibian artists, and the permanent

Rock engravings of wildlife subjects in Twyfelfontein

collection at the National Art Gallery of Namibia, which dates from the mid-19th century, reflects the country's slogan 'Unity in Diversity'.

Crafts

Traditional African crafts include wood carving, basket making, leatherwork, beadwork and pottery, with the contemporary additions of textiles, embroidery and weaving. The vibrant Namibia Crafts Centre in Windhoek is a great place to get an overview. There are craft and curio markets in many places around the country and a growing number of small traditional crafts projects and co-operatives that bring employment and an income to needy communities.

The northern Kavango people are skilled woodcarvers. Their markets in Okahandja north of Windhoek are a convenient location to purchase their myriad animal carvings, wooden bowls and spoons, headrests, drums, toys, boxes, tables, walking sticks and masks.

The Himba and San peoples are famed for their beadwork, the Himba for their use of iron beads and shells, the San for the combination of porcupine quills, seeds, nuts and strings of carved ostrich shell beads. Both use beads to decorate their leatherwork, from bags and pouches to headbands and belts.

Traditionally, baskets have been made by weaving strips of makalani palm leaves into a variety of shapes and sizes depending on what they will be used for. Winnowing grain demands a large, flat, circular shape, while baskets for carrying things are bowl-like in form. Geometric patterns are woven into the baskets using strips of palm leaves dyed dark brown, purple or yellow.

Hand-woven wall hangings and rugs are highlights of the contemporary crafts scene. Using the spun and dyed wool of hardy karakul sheep, the designs tend to feature Namibian landscapes, animals and birds, or modern geometric and abstract patterns, but any design can be commissioned. There are weavers' workshops in Swakopmund and the small town of Dordabis south of Windhoek.

Skilled Nama needlewomen create appliquéd wall hangings portraying animals and scenes of village life, attractive cushion covers and embroidered household linens of the highest quality. The delightful dolls crafted by Herero women, dressed in clothes that date back to Victorian missionary days, are favourite buys for tourists, as are the many and varied creations by township wire-and-tin artists. Modern jewellers use precious metals and gemstones in ever more inventive designs, while potters and ceramic artists are incorporating African and European traditions into their work.

Music

From the trance dancing of the earliest San (Bushmen), music, song and dance have always played a central role in the community life of Namibian peoples. Musical instruments range from the simplest of reed flutes, gourd hand rattles and horn trumpets to various types of drums and stringed instruments.

Missionaries established religious choral groups and, as a result of the years under colonial and apartheid rule, there is a strong European musical tradition. Namibia has a National Symphony Orchestra and a National Youth Choir and theatres host classical ballet and opera performances.

In the townships, where rap, hip-hop, *kwaito* and funky *mbaganga* music from South Africa, and Owambo *oviritije* singers such as Ambros Kaakunga are popular, music often addresses current social problems such as HIV/AIDS and alcohol and drug abuse, getting across a message that can otherwise be difficult to deliver. Namibian Afro-reggae singer-songwriter Ras Sheehama has appeared in European clubs and festivals and toured in the USA.

It is the choirs that have had the most success internationally, in particular the innovative Unam Choir of the University of Namibia. Singing in the African tradition, a cappella, in all Namibia's European and African languages, their varied repertoire includes religious, concert, traditional and folk music. The Mascato Coastal Youth Choir and Walvis Bay Marimba Band are excellent, too.

Festivals

The annual summer Bank Windhoek Arts Festival held in September and October, which began in 2003, proved so successful that a winter festival in June and July was added in 2007. Celebrating all aspects of the arts, from painting and pottery, photography and poetry to music, dance and theatre, participants come from all over the country. The festival also sponsors cultural activities throughout the year and commissions new theatre work. (*www.bankwindhoekarts.com.na*)

The Wild Cinema International Film Festival held annually in Windhoek showcases new work by Namibian filmmakers as well as screening feature and documentary films from around the world.

Culture

A local singing group entertain at Klein Aus Vista

Peoples of Namibia

Namibia's population is made up of 11 main ethnic groups and many different cultures living peacefully together. Between them they speak 28 languages or major dialects.

Basters

Afrikaans-speaking people of mixed race, these predominantly farming people with a strong sense of identity moved up from the Cape in South Africa, founding the town of Rehoboth in 1871.

Bushmen (San)

Living in small communities on the edge of the Kalahari Desert, they are descendants of the earliest hunter-gatherer people who lived in Namibia many thousands of years ago. Small and slight in stature, with pale golden skin, almond-shaped eyes and high cheekbones, they speak a sophisticated language of click sounds.

Caprivian

Members of several different tribes living at the eastern end of the fertile Caprivi Strip, Caprivians raise cattle, grow crops, fish and are renowned for their basketry, woven mats, weaving and pottery.

Coloured Namibians

Descendants of mixed African and European origin, coloured Namibians were restricted to their own townships, schools and churches during the apartheid years and they have a strong sense of their own identity and culture. They generally speak Afrikaans and live mainly in urban areas in central and southern Namibia.

Damara

Among the earliest inhabitants of Namibia, Damara speak a 'click' language similar to that of the Bushmen. Traditionally farmers and skilled smelters, Damara people are found in all walks of life, including government.

Herero

Skilled at raising cattle, the Herero were originally pastoralists who settled in Kaokoland and moved south. Herero women are famous for their colourful Victorian-style dress of long voluminous skirts and headdresses twisted to resemble the horns of a cow. Introduced by German missionaries' wives, it has become their traditional dress and is worn with pride.

Himba

The Himba split from the main group of Hereros in the 19th century and live very traditional lives raising cattle in the remote and arid Kaokoland. They eschew modern dress and are a source of fascination to social anthropologists and photographers.

Kavango

Agriculture and fishing are the main occupations of the people who live on the border with Angola alongside the Okavango River, from which they take their name. They are also skilled woodcarvers and sell their work at markets and curio shops all over the country. During the Angolan civil war, so many Kavango moved across the border that this group is now the second-largest in Namibia.

Nama

The earliest Namibians after the Bushmen, with whom they share a similar 'clicking' language, the Nama were semi-nomadic pastoralists who lost their traditional lands in the 19th and 20th centuries. They mainly work on commercial farms in the south of the country.

Owambo

Twelve tribes make up this large ethnic group that represents over half

Himba people still live in traditional ways

of the population of Namibia. The Owambo live mainly in the fertile far north of the country where they farm livestock and crops and are traders and business people. The South African administration used them as a source of contract workers for the mines, and the governing SWAPO party grew out of the Owamboland People's Organisation, which was formed to fight the hated system.

White Namibians

The first white settlers were Germans and farmers of Dutch origin from South Africa. Under South African rule most viable commercial farming land was transferred into Afrikaner ownership and the system of apartheid ensured the economy was firmly in white hands. The population numbers around 100,000.

Highlights

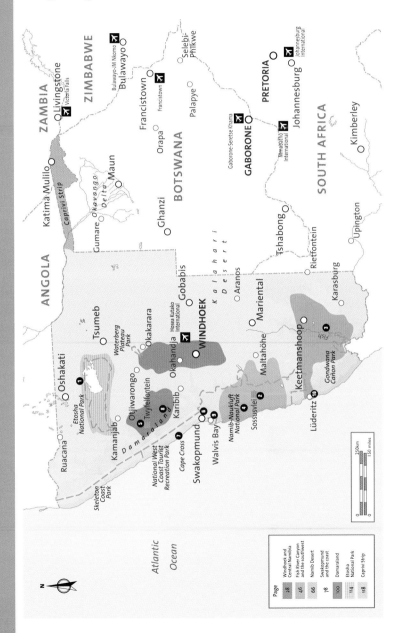

Page

28   Windhoek and
      Central Namibia

46   Fish River Canyon
      and the southwest

66   Namib Desert

78   Swakopmund
      and the coast

100   Damaraland

114   Etosha
      National Park

118   Caprivi Strip

❶ Etosha National Park Spot lion, elephant, leopard, black rhino, giraffe, zebra, myriad birds and so much more – this is one of the world's great conservation areas.

❷ Sossusvlei Marvel at the sinuous shapes of the towering desert dunes and the way light plays on the orange-red sand.

❸ Fish River Canyon Look in awe at the sheer size and scale of 'Africa's Grand Canyon'.

❹ Namib-Naukluft National Park Be intrigued by the creatures and plants that survive in the desert, like the strange, tangled *Welwitschia mirabilis* that lives for hundreds of years.

❺ Twyfelfontein View one of the largest collections of rock engravings in Africa, a picture book of animals incised 6,000 years ago.

❻ Swakopmund Thrill to quad biking or sand boarding in the nearby dunes, and shop for arts and crafts amid the colonial architecture of Namibia's summer playground.

❼ Cape Cross Be captivated by the antics of 100,000 Cape fur seals that live, breed and squabble noisily in this coastal reserve.

❽ Damaraland Search for the elusive desert-adapted elephants that roam the dry Huab riverbed and surrounding bush.

❾ Walvis Bay View vast flocks of flamingos feeding in the lagoon that's home to 80 different bird species.

❿ Lüderitz Feast on rock lobster in this laid-back town of German *Jugendstil* houses along the diamond coast.

Endangered blue cranes can be seen in the Etosha National Park

Suggested itineraries

Namibia is a vast country with so much to see and do that it can be hard to know where to start. But whether you have just a few days, a week or two, or much longer, you can be sure of myriad unforgettable experiences. View big game from your car, walk in the bush or hike through mountains, watch the play of sun and shadow across towering desert dunes, see night skies with more stars than you'd ever dreamed possible – and let the wide-open spaces capture your imagination.

Long weekend

From the capital, Windhoek, it's possible to see some of the world's greatest natural sights in just a few days. Drive north for five hours and you're in the Etosha National Park, one of Africa's biggest conservation areas and home to millions of animals. Drive south for a similar distance and the sea of towering dunes at Sossusvlei will leave you mesmerised. If you don't feel like driving, book a weekend package tour or join one of the small group tours by light aircraft. These will have you at your destination in no time, with some great aerial views of the landscape to add to the adventure.

Etosha has countless kilometres of well-kept gravel roads, so you can spend your days on your own personal safari, watching wildlife from your car window. As night falls, there's nothing quite like enjoying a barbecue under the stars knowing that great herds of animals are sharing their habitat with you, or relaxing with a sundowner by a waterhole when elephant families arrive for their evening drink. Keep watch by a floodlit waterhole and there's a good chance you'll see black rhino. There are three rest camps with restaurants, offering the choice of staying in elegantly appointed rooms or campsites.

Outside the park gates, smart private lodges bring comfort and style to the bush. They have their own vehicles for game drives and rangers to take you on bush walks. Everything is taken care of on a fly-in safari to one of these lodges.

Christus Kirche in Windhoek, a historic Lutheran church

A wild teak tree brings brilliant colour to the dry bush of northern Namibia

Sossusvlei is a very special place and a highlight of Namibia's many grand sights. The towering desert dunes, up to 375m (1,230ft) high, form a dramatic contrast with the clay pan at their feet. Drive there, take an organised tour, or book a fly-in safari with one of the luxury lodges in the area.

Just an hour's flight from Windhoek's Eros airport, Swakopmund is a great short-break destination. This quirky town on the coast is a summer retreat for locals living in the interior of the country. Known as Namibia's 'adventure capital' for such activities as sand boarding and quad biking in the nearby dunes, it's a relaxed place with interesting colonial architecture, good restaurants and an abundance of African art and curio shops. Numerous tour operators offer trips down to Walvis Bay for dolphin-watching cruises and birding on the lagoon, up to Cape Cross to the see the big colony of Cape fur seals and into the Namib-Naukluft National Park, so there's no need to hire a car unless you want to.

One week

Distances between sights are long, and although there are tour operators that will show you the classic highlights of Namibia in a week, it will necessarily be a rushed and tiring trip by land, and expensive by air. While it may seem tempting to cram in as much as possible, giving yourself more time in an area increases your enjoyment of the holiday.

The international airport is at Windhoek, a city that's well worth a day of your time on arrival or departure.

Suggested itineraries

Okavango River

From there, the country divides rather neatly into two circuits: northern Namibia and southern Namibia. Either of these routes could form the basis of a one-week itinerary.

The northern route encompasses the Etosha National Park, the strange landscapes and rock engravings of Damaraland, the Cape fur seal reserve at Cape Cross on the edge of the Skeleton Coast, the coastal town of Swakopmund and the northern part of the Namib-Naukluft National Park where the extraordinary plant *Welwitschia mirabilis* survives for centuries on the gravel desert plains.

The southern route offers the Namib-Naukluft National Park with the grandiose dunes at Sossusvlei, the red-earthed Kalahari, the awesome Fish River Canyon, often called 'Africa's Grand Canyon', and Lüderitz, an old German town on the diamond coast.

Two weeks

Packing the northern and southern routes into two weeks is possible, and many travel companies offer itineraries that include most or all of the main sights. Hiring a car obviously gives you the freedom to tailor the trip to suit your interests.

Namibia has good asphalt roads and the network of gravel roads is generally kept in good condition, but don't expect fast motorways and don't plan to drive at night. It is important to be at your destination by sunset, as animals have a habit of suddenly appearing out of nowhere after dark.

Try to arrange to stay at least two days in each region you visit. To see the dunes in the early morning light and at sunset is to experience the true magic of Sossusvlei. A two- or three-night stay in Swakopmund would give you time to enjoy the town, try some of the adventure activities, get to Walvis Bay for a boat trip and birdwatching on the lagoon, or perhaps take a sightseeing flight over the Skeleton Coast. The Fish River Canyon may feel a long way south, but it is an incredible sight.

If viewing wildlife is a priority, three days in Etosha and a stay on one of the many private game farms would be an important part of your itinerary. Okonjima Lodge, home of the AfriCat Foundation, is memorable. If you are returning from the northern circuit en route for Windhoek and your flight home, a night or two there is a wonderful way to end your holiday.

Longer

With three weeks or more you could allow more time at each destination to explore the region in greater depth. Or, after seeing the highlights of southern and northern Namibia, continue northeast from Etosha via Grootfontein to Rundu near the border with Angola, where the landscape changes dramatically and the area feels a lot more 'African'. The banks of the Okavango River are lush and green.

The rivers and waterfalls of the Caprivi Strip come as a surprising contrast to the arid lands you have previously travelled through, there's plenty of game and birdlife in the reserves and quiet sunset cruises on pontoons from the lodges. You could drive across the border into Botswana for game viewing in Chobe National Park or into Zambia to visit the spectacular Victoria Falls.

The oryx, known as gemsbok locally, are a common sight in Etosha National Park

Windhoek and central Namibia

At the head of a long valley 1,650m (5,415ft) above sea level and surrounded by hills and mountains, Namibia's capital, Windhoek, sits on the central highlands at the geographical heart of the country. The only proclaimed city, it is the centre of government and home to around 234,000 people, which makes it one of the world's smallest capitals. Yet the number of its residents constitutes about 13 per cent of the entire population of Namibia.

International flights land at Hosea Kutako International Airport, 42km (26 miles) to the east. It's a scenic drive into town along a fine road that winds through mountains where wildlife is often spotted. Windhoek's second and smaller airport, Eros, lies closer to the city to the south and handles mainly light aircraft and internal flights by Air Namibia.

Windhoek is a clean and pleasant city with some interesting architecture, museums and art galleries and good shops and restaurants. It is well worth a day of your time at the beginning or end of the holiday.

Heading north from Windhoek, the B1 road passes through cattle-ranching country and some of the Khomas Hochland mountains that stretch all the way west to the Namib Desert. After 72km (45 miles), the huge woodcarvers' market at Okahandja seems a good reason to break the journey to the Waterberg Plateau Park, which shelters rare and endangered animals within its amphitheatre of high sandstone cliffs, or to one of the superb lodges that offer close encounters with leopard, cheetah and lion.

South of Windhoek lie Lake Oanob, which is the highest dam in Namibia, and the grassy plains, acacia woodlands, rolling dunes and sweeping red sands of the Kalahari Desert.

WINDHOEK

The commercial centre of Windhoek may seem small when compared with capital cities elsewhere, but its wide streets lined with German colonial architecture, modern office blocks, department stores and shopping malls contain everything the visitor needs, from good hotels and restaurants to banks, theatres and safari outfitters. It feels very European, but the crafts sellers, who line the pavement opposite leafy Zoo Park on Independence Avenue and lay out their wares among the stores and cafés along Post Street Mall, tell you that this is definitely Africa.

Modern Windhoek was officially born in 1890 when the Schutztruppe (German colonial troops) under Major Curt von François began building the Alte Feste (Old Fortress), which now houses an excellent museum. But the area was inhabited long before that, due to the existence of hot springs in what is now the upmarket suburb of Klein-Windhoek. The Nama people called it /Ae-//Gams meaning 'firewater' (the // symbols indicate a click sound in the Nama language) and the Herero people knew it as Otjomuise ('place of steam'). The Oorlam people, led by Jan Jonker Afrikaner, settled there in the 1840s and built up a busy trading centre.

Alongside the new modern buildings, it's the early 20th-century German architecture that helps to give central Windhoek its European atmosphere – including the buildings with pitched roofs designed to shrug off snow! You'll see them on Independence Avenue, the main shopping thoroughfare, but they are at their most impressive lining the hill overlooking the central business district.

Ideally, time your visit for during the week. Although a few shops open on Sunday, essentially the city closes down from around 1pm on Saturday until Monday morning. Many restaurants are closed on Sundays.

The streets are busy but not frenetic and there's an air of organised efficiency about the shops and businesses. It's easy to relax and forget that cosmopolitan Windhoek is a city

and that crime does happen. It's wise to keep a firm hand on handbags and belongings and take a taxi in the

evenings. If you are driving, ensure that your hotel or guesthouse has secure off-street parking.

Windhoek Tourist Information Bureau *Post Street Mall. Tel: (061) 290 2092/2401. www.windhoekcc.org.na*

Tourist Information Kiosk *Independence Ave, opposite the Kalahari Sands Hotel.*

Alte Feste (Old Fort)

Windhoek's oldest building, completed in 1892, houses good displays that explore Namibia's colonial and recent history, including photographs of important Namibian leaders and significant events, and early household equipment and furniture used by missionaries and settlers which contrast with those used by indigenous Namibian peoples. The Independence Exhibition vividly tells the story of years of struggle in the liberation war with South Africa and the transition to majority rule. Namibia's prehistoric rock art is also explored and explained.

Display at the Alte Feste Museum

Robert Mugabe Ave. Tel: (061) 276 800. Open: 9am–6pm (summer); 9am–5pm (winter). Closed: public holidays. Free admission, but donations welcomed.

Christus Kirche (Christ Church)

The oldest Evangelical Lutheran church in Namibia, it's an attractive landmark building with a slim tower, gabled front and Art Nouveau influences. The stained-glass windows, donated by Kaiser Wilhelm II, are particularly fine. Consecrated in 1910, it was supposed to celebrate peace between the German, Owambo, Herero and Nama peoples and contains plaques to the German soldiers who died in the various wars and uprisings.

Corner Fidel Castro St & Robert Mugabe Ave. For opening hours, check with the Windhoek Tourist Information Centre (Tel: (061) 290 2092).

Gibeon Meteorite fountain

Some 30 600-million-year-old meteorites are mounted on steel columns to create a sculptural fountain in the open-air centre of pedestrian Post Street Mall. Composed mainly of iron, with an average weight of over 300kg (660lb), they are part of what is believed to be the world's heaviest shower of meteorites and were found near Gibeon, south of Windhoek.

Namibia Crafts Centre

High-quality, fairly traded crafts from all over Namibia are displayed in over 30 stalls on two floors of a former

The Gibeon Meteorite fountain, centrepiece of Windhoek's Post Street shopping mall

brewery. There's everything here, from fun wire animals to exquisite beading and embroidery, traditionally dressed Herero dolls to cheerful fabrics and plenty of treats for the home including fine linens, ceramics, superb baskets and handwoven rugs. The Ombo Art Gallery, with work by Namibian artists, is also in this building. It's a bright and colourful place with a good café and an Internet point.

40 Tal St. Tel: (061) 242 222.
Open: Mon–Fri 9am–5.30pm, Sat, Sun
& public holidays 9am–1.30pm.

National Art Gallery of Namibia

A fairly small but interesting gallery that houses the country's biggest permanent collection of Namibian art from the 19th and 20th centuries. It also hosts changing contemporary exhibitions.

Corner Robert Mugabe Ave & John
Meinert St. Tel: (061) 231 160. Open:
Tue–Fri 9am–5pm, Sat 9am–2pm.
Donations welcomed.

St George's Cathedral

Built in 1924 for the Anglican community, this is the smallest functioning cathedral in southern Africa. Its brown bricks and exposed beams give it a decidedly English feel, complemented by the bell in the tower which comes from a set cast in 1670 for St Mary's Church in Canterbury.

Corner Love St & Sinclair Rd. Open: for
services. For opening hours, check with
the Windhoek Tourist Information
Centre (Tel: (061) 290 2092).

The National Art Gallery has a permanent collection of Namibian art and hosts changing exhibitions

Tintenpalast

Namibia's parliament sits in this lovely old two-storey building set in colourful landscaped gardens. Completed in 1914, it was built to house the German colonial government. It was then used by the South African administration until independence, when it was renovated. The name means 'Ink Palace', which is said to refer to the excessive quantity of ink used by the bureaucrats.

Robert Mugabe Ave. Tel: tour bookings (061) 202 8097/8062. Open: guided tours Mon–Fri (excluding public holidays) 9–10am, 10–11am & 3–4pm.

TransNamib Museum

On the first floor of the historic railway station building, a collection of models and memorabilia reflects the progress of transport in Namibia, particularly the railways, from 1895. The collection includes wooden cupboards used to store and display tickets, electrical communication equipment, historical maps and drawings, railway timetables and cutlery and crockery used in trains in the German and South African eras. One small room has been transformed into the interior of an old train compartment complete with original washbasin and linen. An Illing locomotive, manufactured in Germany and commissioned during 1904 in Swakopmund, stands outside the building.

Corner Bahnhof St & Mandume Ndemufayo Ave. Tel: (061) 298 2186. Open: Mon–Fri 8am–1pm & 2–5pm. Admission charge.

Zoo Park

A green space right in the centre of the city, Zoo Park has a landscaped garden, pond, children's playground and a Chinese pavilion. Look for the column carved with scenes of an elephant kill that was believed to have taken place on the site about 5,000 years ago. Various Stone Age implements, together with the fossilised bones of two elephants, were discovered there in 1962.

From the park, look back across Independence Avenue to where three attractive German colonial buildings stand out among modern shops. **Gathemann House** was built in 1913 for Heinrich Gathemann, the then mayor of Klein Windhoek, and is now a rather good restaurant (*see p159*). To its right, the **Erkrathus** building dates from 1910 and typically for this

period had living accommodation above the street-level shop. **Kronprinz** to the left, its date 1902 carved into stone, was a hotel.
Independence Ave.

(*see p159*).

CAPITAL FESTIVALS

Windhoek holds two traditional German festivals every year. The WIKA carnival in April sees cabaret evenings, an all-night masked ball and a colourful parade of floats down Independence Avenue. Large amounts of beer and sausages are consumed at Oktoberfest, held at the Sports Club in October, alongside brass bands, games and children's entertainment.

Students from the Polytechnic of Namibia hold a Cultural Week in August, with live bands, traditional costumes, food, talent competitions and gospel shows. University (UNAM) students follow suit with their Cultural Week in September, which is also the month of the /Ae//Gams Festival showcasing Namibian arts and culture with music, dance, poetry and theatre performances.

Windhoek and central Namibia

Tintenpalast, Namibia's historic parliament building, is surrounded by gardens and open for tours

Walk: Windhoek highlights

The centre of Namibia's clean and attractive capital is quite small and its highlights can be seen on a pleasant walk. Plan to set out before 10am or after 3pm when it's cooler.

Allow two or three hours for the 4 km (2½ mile) walk.

Starting at the Windhoek Information kiosk by the car park on Independence Avenue, cross the street to look in the Gustav Voigts shopping centre under the high-rise Kalahari Sands Hotel. Continue south on Independence Avenue and turn right on Sam Nujoma Drive.

1 Namibia Crafts Centre

Passing Bastion 1, which was the headquarters of the South African forces and is now the Ministry of Defence, turn left into Tal Street, where you'll see the popular Warehouse Theatre and the Namibia Crafts Centre. It's packed with some of the best-quality and most imaginative crafts.
Go left up Garten St and left again into Independence Ave. At Sam Nujoma Drive, turn right and then turn left on Robert Mugabe Ave.

2 Alte Feste (Old Fort)

As you walk up the hill past the City Hall, look over to the Auas Mountains to the south, where Moltkeblick, at 2,483m (8,146ft), is the second-highest peak in Namibia. At the traffic lights, go left onto Robert Mugabe Avenue to see the distinctive, white-painted old fortress, the Alte Feste. It houses the National Museum's excellent displays on the history of Namibia and well-presented information on the country's rock art.
Continue north on Robert Mugabe Ave, passing around the back of the Christus Kirche to the gardens of the parliament building.

3 Tintenpalast (Parliament building)

The name means 'Ink Palace' and refers to the bureaucracy emanating from this impressive old colonial building that has housed governments since the early 20th century. Now independent Namibia's parliament, it is set in colourful gardens.
Walk over to the church, which occupies an island in the middle of the road.

4 Christus Kirche (Christ Church)

Built from local sandstone, this pretty 'gingerbread' church with Art Nouveau influences was consecrated in 1910. The stained-glass windows were donated by Kaiser Wilhelm II, the altar Bible by his wife, Augusta.

Walk west downhill along Fidel Castro St.

5 Crafts and Zoo Park

Crafts sellers display woodcarvings, jewellery and baskets at the corner of Fidel Castro St and Independence Avenue. Opposite them, leafy Zoo Park has palm trees, lawns, a Chinese pavilion and an Elephant Column that marks the place where 5,000-year-old fossilised elephant remains and Stone Age tools were discovered.

Go right (north) on Independence Ave for a short distance until you see the replica Clock Tower indicating the top of Post Street Mall.

6 Post Street Mall

Shops and restaurants line this pedestrian street with an outdoor crafts market down the centre. The star attraction here is the Meteorite Fountain, a sculpture made from 600-million-year old meteorite fragments found in southern Namibia in 1911.

Return down Independence Ave to your starting point. Along the way, if you turn right down Fidel Castro St you can call in at the Namibia Tourist Board offices, which provide a good selection of country maps and information.

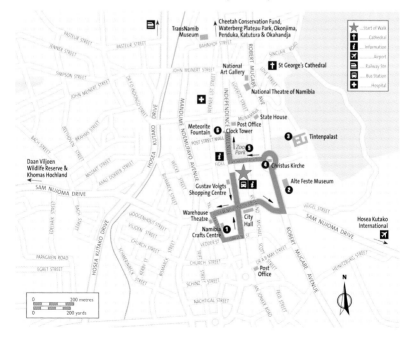

AROUND WINDHOEK
Cheetah Conservation Fund

You get a view of the Waterberg Plateau (*see pp38–9*) from the verandah at CCF Namibia, the headquarters of a non-profit organisation that focuses on cheetah research and conservation. Graphics, panels and interactive displays give an insight into these magnificent animals, Africa's most endangered cat species. Namibia has the largest and healthiest population of cheetahs left in the world, and CCF is working to keep it that way.

The centre has a garden, gift shop and small coffee shop. Visitors can also watch cheetahs being fed, usually around 2pm on weekdays and Saturday at noon, but phone to check on the day.

On the D2440, about 44km (27 miles) east of Otjiwarongo. Tel: (067) 306 225. www.cheetah.org. Open: 9am–5pm. Admission by minimum donation.

Daan Viljoen Wildlife Reserve

A popular local picnic spot and camping site with a swimming pool, this national park lying west of Windhoek has walking trails amid the rolling dry scrub landscape. Game to be spotted includes kudu, blue wildebeest, Hartmann's mountain zebra, oryx, klipspringer and springbok as well as numerous birds. Over 200 species have been recorded in the park, including brightly coloured rollers and bee-eaters, distinctive hornbills, noisy white-tailed shrikes and the aptly named Damara

rockjumper. Waterbirds congregate by the small Augeigas Dam.

There's a 6km (4 mile) game drive – a one-way route marked as 'Detour' – with viewpoints, but the easy 3km (2 mile) Wag-'n-bietjie walking trail could possibly result in more game sightings and there's the sense of being out in the bush yet only a short distance from the city. The trail's name is Afrikaans for 'wait a bit' and comes from the common name for the buffalo thorn tree that has curved, backward-pointing thorns on its branches. When these catch on clothing it's necessary to wait while you detach

See wildlife close to the city at Daan Viljoen Wildlife Reserve

yourself. There are plenty of these trees around, so be warned. The trail follows the Augeigas River upstream to a lookout point above the Stengel Dam. The park has two other trails, the more strenuous and hilly Rooibos (red bushwillow) at 9km (6 miles) long, and the Sweet-Thorn, which is 32km (20 miles), takes two days and must be booked in advance.

The park lies among the rolling schist hills of the Khomas Hochland. Three steep and very scenic passes cross the hills, then drop abruptly down into the vast plains of the Namib Desert.
Daan Viljoen Game Park is 30km (19 miles) west of Windhoek in the Khomas Hochland hills.
Tel: (061) 230 955. Open: sunrise–sunset. Admission charge.

Katutura

In 1959, as part of South Africa's apartheid policy, black Namibians were forcibly removed from Windhoek to townships outside the city. Katutura ('the place where we cannot settle') was the largest of these. Today, it is a sprawling suburb bigger than central Windhoek, has houses that range from smart and expensive abodes to corrugated-iron shacks, and is a vibrant place with bars, restaurants and two big traditional African markets. An organised township tour is a worthwhile and interesting experience. Particularly recommended is **Katutura Face to Face Tours** (*Tel: (061) 265 446*). *10km (6 miles) north of Windhoek.*

Okahandja

The daily, huge, open-air woodcarvers market (*see p140*) on the northern side of town is the main reason for stopping at Okahandja – be prepared to bargain! The administrative centre for the Herero people, Okahandja is at the junction of routes heading north to the Waterberg Plateau and Etosha National Parks and west to Swakopmund and the coast.

Several important Herero chiefs are buried in Okahandja, and two processions in which Herero people honour their forefathers and leaders take place here annually in June and August. With the women dressed in their traditional Victorian dresses and men in military uniforms, they are colourful occasions.
70km (44 miles) north of Windhoek.

Dinosaur footprints

Tracks of a two-legged, three-toed dinosaur can be seen in sandstone rock on Otjihaenamaparero, a guest farm with camping facilities. Declared a National Monument in 1951, the cluster of shallow indentations is estimated to be 150 to 185 million years old.
North of Okahandja, off the D2414 towards Kalkfeld. Tel: (067) 290 153. www.dinosaurstracks.com. Admission charge.

Okonjima

Of the many guest farms in the area, Okonjima stands out. It is home to the AfriCat Foundation (*see pp44–5*) and

Get close-up encounters with cheetah at Okonjima

activities for its guests include tracking leopard and cheetah and close-up encounters with the big cats, including lion. On a night visit to a hide, you're likely to see porcupine and honey badger. The accommodation (*see p161*) is luxuriously comfortable. It is not open to day visitors but a night or two here will send you home with memories that last a lifetime.
Okonjima is 220km (137 miles) north of Windhoek.

Penduka

The name means 'wake up' in the Oshiwambo and Otjiherero languages. This development project works with disadvantaged but highly skilled women who make top-quality, stylish table and bed linen, batik and embroidery, and glass-bead jewellery from discarded broken bottles. The

beautiful designs for the fabrics are based on bird and animal motifs and link oral traditions, narrative depictions of rural life and visual arts. The project provides a cash income for about 400 women working from home in often isolated locations and their work is put together in the workshop, which is a friendly and fascinating place to visit.

About 7km (4 miles) from Windhoek city centre, the Penduka workshop is by the Goreangab Dam beyond Katutura. As well as having an attractive shop, which also sells work by other community-based projects in Namibia, and a café, it also offers simple but comfortable lakeside accommodation. *Penduka is 7km (4 miles) northwest of the city centre. Signed from Green Mountain Dam Rd. Tel: (061) 257 210. www.penduka.com. Open: Mon–Sat 8am–5pm.*

Waterberg Plateau Park

A vast amphitheatre of sheer, lichen-streaked, red-sandstone cliffs, formed 200 million years ago, rises some 200m (660ft) out of flat plains that stretch to the horizon. Its forested slopes are home to a wide variety of animals, from giraffe, kudu, rare rhino and tsessebe, an antelope, to playful mongooses that skitter on the rest-camp lawns and the chacma baboons with a penchant for emptying rubbish bins. Hornbills croak in the trees, black eagles soar overhead and squabbling francolins are nature's morning wake-up call.

MOPANE TREES

The versatile mopane tree (*Colophospermum mopane*) grows widely in Namibia's north. Elephants eat its bark and twigs and its leaves are used for medicinal purposes. When the dried leaves fall to the ground they provide phosphorus, and protein-rich food for animals. The wood of the mopane tree is used in ritual ceremonies and for the Himba's sacred fire. Owambo people make rope from mopane bark, clean their teeth with its twigs, hollow out the bark for troughs, burn it as firewood for cooking and producing charcoal and make their homes and furniture from its wood. Mopane worms, the caterpillars that live on its branches, are dried or grilled to make tasty treats rich in protein.

The park was created as a sanctuary for rare and endangered animals in 1972 and to explore it you have to either take one of the organised game drives or hike. There are several marked walking trails, of varying length, all easily accessed from the rest camp (*see Directory, p161*), including one to the top of the plateau from where there are spectacular views. The park also organises wilderness trails lasting several days. The plateau is 50km (31 miles) by 16km (10 miles) and in the early morning light the red sandstone rock glows a fiery red, a vibrant contrast to the green of the trees, bush and tall grasses.

Waterberg was where the decisive battle between the Herero people and the German colonists took place on 11 August 1904. Superior firepower pushed the Herero east into the Kalahari, and over the following months thousands of men, women and children, and their cattle, died of starvation during their long trek into exile.

Waterberg Plateau Park is 300km (186 miles) northeast of Windhoek. From the B1 main road north of Windhoek, turn right onto the C22 and left onto the D2512. It is well signposted.
www.nwr.com.na

The towering sandstone cliffs of the Waterberg Plateau Park glow red in the early morning sunlight

Townships

In post-independence Namibia, the term 'township' may seem odd, a remnant of the apartheid era when people were segregated on grounds of race and the life of anyone not classified a 'white' was severely restricted. But the name has stuck.

Originally known as 'Locations', these residential areas of basic housing with virtually no facilities were planned and built as labour dormitories, far from the centre of town and the white residential suburbs. Every town, however small, had one. Rows of uniform, shoe-box houses lined dirt roads, and residents were not allowed to own property or start businesses – even shops – there.

Today, townships are still home to the majority of black and mixed-race Namibians in the central and southern regions, though as towns have grown they have become more akin to suburbs and look entirely different. There are some very grand and expensive homes in Windhoek's sprawling Katutura Township, as well as acres of informal settlements of shacks that accommodate ever more people from rural areas in search of work.

In 1959, people who since 1913 had been living in the 'Old Location' on the edge of Windhoek, began to be forcibly removed to a bleak area northwest of the city. They named it Katutura, a Herero word variously translated as 'we have no dwelling place' and 'the place we do not want to stay'. Opposition to the move was ruthlessly crushed. On 10 December 1959, 11 people were shot dead, 44 required medical attention and many more were injured in clashes with the police. The date is fixed in the Namibian calendar as Human Rights Day.

Not only were people of differently coloured skins required to live separately, they had to live within their own ethnic group. Hence areas were sectioned off for Hereros, Damaras, Namas and so on. Owambo contract workers were housed in a separate 'compound'.

In Swakopmund the move out to Mondesa Township was quiet. Seeing what had happened in Windhoek, although angered by their forced removal, the people decided to move peacefully.

Sited on the edge of the desert, Mondesa's residents have to deal with wind, fog and sand, but their neat houses, many colourfully painted and with small gardens, have an air of pride about them. There's a great sense of community spirit.

An informal settlement has grown up near the dunes where people live and wait hopefully for a home in the main township. Known as the Democratic Resettlement Community (the DRC), it is well organised, but the shacks put together mainly from finds in the nearby municipal rubbish dump ('the DRC hardware store') have pit latrines and no electricity. Yet even there, each home has been stamped with the owner's personality, often decorated quite ingeniously.

You can go on organised township tours in both Katutura and Mondesa and they are great experiences. People are very welcoming, children clamour to be photographed, you get to meet some fascinating residents, drink in a local bar, eat traditional foods and learn a lot.

Hata Angu Cultural Tours, Swakopmund. Tel: (064) 404 016. Katutura Face to Face Tours, Windhoek. Tel: (061) 265 446. www.face2facetours.com

Katutura is home to a large number of Windhoek's residents

Drive: South of Windhoek

The long straight road south has vistas of the purple Auas Mountains and passes through a landscape of ochre earth, low scrub and farms where cattle, sheep and goats are raised. The rolling red dunes of the Kalahari Desert and a stylish wilderness lodge beckon.

You can use this 175km (109 mile) route as a two-day round trip from Windhoek or as the start of a journey south towards the Fish River Canyon.

Leave Windhoek on the B1, the main road south, towards Rehoboth.

1 Heroes Acre

A memorial constructed in 2002, it recognises the people's long struggle for independence, freedom and democracy. Set in 735ha (1,816 acres) of land, it has bronze statues, and a large wall panel depicting historical uprisings and the liberation war.
Continue on the B1 towards Rehoboth. After about 79km (49 miles), turn off

right onto the gravel road D1237, signed Lake Oanob.

2 Lake Oanob

A dam created in 1990, Lake Oanob is set among mountains, bush and rocky outcrops with an attractive resort that welcomes day visitors as well as overnighters. A thatched restaurant overlooks the blue lake water and children's swimming pool, and there are nature trails and boats for hire. A peaceful spot to the west of Rehoboth,

Red sand is characteristic of the Kalahari Desert in Namibia

it's a pleasant place to take a break on the journey.

www.oanob.com.na

Return to the B1, turning south for Rehoboth.

3 Rehoboth

This neat little town is the centre of the fiercely independent, Afrikaans-speaking Baster community. People of mixed race, they moved up from the Cape in South Africa, founding Rehoboth in 1871. A small museum in the old Postmaster's House next to the post office tells their story (*Tel: (0627) 522 954. www.rehobothmuseum.com. Open: Mon–Fri 9am–noon & 2–4pm, Sat 9am–noon*).

Continue south on the B1.

4 Tropic of Capricorn

About 10km (6 miles) out of Rehoboth the road crosses the Tropic of Capricorn. Stop for a photo opportunity.

Continue south on the B1 to Kalkrand. Turn left (east) on the gravel road C21 and drive into the Kalahari Desert.

5 Kalahari Desert

Long ridges of tree-dotted red sand dunes separated by grassy valleys distinguish the Kalahari landscape, which is arid but not a 'true' desert as it receives more than 100mm (4in) of rain a year. Camelthorn trees weighed down with the massive nests of sociable weaver birds line the road.

Turn right (south) onto the D1268.

6 Intu Afrika Kalahari Game Reserve

Three superb lodges (*see pp160–61*) on a 10,000ha (24,710 acre) reserve make a great wilderness experience. On an evening game drive you are likely to see giraffe, oryx, wildebeest, zebra and even a bat-eared fox, as well as the three rescued Kalahari lions. Don't miss an early morning walk with !Xoo Bushmen, who reveal facets of their traditional life as hunter-gatherers.

Return to Windhoek, or continue on your journey south.

The AfriCat Foundation

Namibia is home to approximately 25 per cent of the world's cheetah population, most of which live on farmland. Inevitably there are conflicts between humans and the big cats and the AfriCat Foundation started off in 1993 as a sanctuary for cheetah and leopard rescued from irate livestock farmers. Today, this non-profit organisation is dedicated to the protection and long-term conservation of all large carnivores in Namibia and runs programmes and projects that encompass research, education and animal welfare. Its pioneering work has earned it numerous international ecological and ecotourism awards.

The aim is to relocate as many animals as possible into the wild or, if they can't be rehabilitated, to give them refuge and care for and feed them in the reserves. It's the world's largest cheetah and leopard rescue and release programme, with well over 900 cats rescued and around 800 released back into their own environment since the project began.

In an average year, AfriCat rescues 70 cheetahs and leopards that have been trapped, injured or orphaned on farms throughout Namibia. Most of those will be released back into their natural environment. The foundation also works with the farmers, sharing knowledge about effective livestock management techniques that can help to minimise their losses.

The reasons why an animal cannot be released into the wild include extensive injuries, they have been in captivity elsewhere and become habituated to humans, or they are cubs too young to cope on their own. Cheetah mothers spend many months teaching their young to hunt, and if the cubs have been captured without their mothers, or the adult cheetah has been killed, they do not have sufficient knowledge or skills to survive for long in the wild.

Cheetahs that have been previously captive are released into the 4,500ha (11,000 acre) Tusk Trust Rehabilitation Park to give them the opportunity to hone their hunting skills. They are fitted with radio collars so they can be closely monitored. When they are considered to be suitably 'bush-wise' they can be relocated to a private game reserve where their progress will continue to be observed.

Leopards are shy, secretive, nocturnal animals that tend to hunt creatures that are the most abundant within their territory. Farmers regularly catch, poison and shoot them to

Radio collars enable the Foundation to monitor the progress of their residents

prevent further livestock losses. There are over 7,000 livestock and game farms in the country and the conflict between predator and farmers protecting their livelihood reduces the natural habitat areas where the animals can safely exist. AfriCat offers to remove leopards and cheetahs from traps, preventing them from being shot.

Although most of the animals cared for on the 22,000ha (55,000 acre) reserve are cheetahs and leopards,

there are also several lions there and a group of wild dogs. AfriCat is successfully combining conservation with tourism. Guests at Okonjima's lodges have the opportunity of tracking and getting close to these magnificent animals in a vast wild and natural environment.

The AfriCat Foundation is based at the guest farm Okonjima, north of Okahandja in central Namibia (see p161). www.africat.org or www.okonjima.com

Fish River Canyon and the southwest

One of Africa's greatest natural wonders, the Fish River Canyon is considered second in size only to Arizona's Grand Canyon and its most spectacular section is the 56km (35 mile) stretch between the southernmost and northernmost viewpoints. The far south and southwest of Namibia is arid and sparsely populated, with long distances between small towns and the main attractions, but there is much to fascinate.

This is a region of tabletop and butte mountains, endless grassy plains, great outcrops of glowing red rock ignited by the setting sun, long dry riverbeds and vast horizons under dazzling blue skies. Three desert systems overlap here, creating a unique flora.

A 'forest' of quiver trees (*Aloe dichotoma*) rises from stony ground and crowns rocky hills near Keetmanshoop. Wild horses, their origins a mystery, roam the desert flatlands beyond Aus. Towards the coast it's diamond country, defined by the desolate expanses of the *Sperrgebiet* ('forbidden area'). Then there's Lüderitz, the quirky German town by the ocean, full of early 20th-century colonial architecture. And Kolmanskop, a ghost mining town abandoned to the desert sand.

Empty roads slice through wide-open spaces backed by distant brown hills and purple mountains. There are sightings of ostrich, oryx and graceful gazelles. Sheep and goats graze on stubbly sun-bleached grass that will suddenly become fields of green when the rain comes. In southwestern Namibia, the desert even blooms. Beige-brown plains burst into shades of bright yellow, pink, purple and blue after the first good winter rain. Less touched by tourism, the 'deep south' of Namibia is made for discovery.

FISH RIVER CANYON

Known as 'Africa's Grand Canyon', the awesome Fish River Canyon has evolved over countless millennia. At 161km (100 miles) long, up to 27km (17 miles) wide and 550m (1,804ft) deep, it vies with Ethiopia's Blue Nile Gorge to be the second-largest canyon on earth. The snaking Fish River flows intermittently, leaving pools of water containing yellowfish, catfish, tilapia and common carp. Ground squirrel, rock hyrax, baboon and klipspringer inhabit the canyon, and leopard tracks are seen at waterholes. Eagles soar overhead.

As with so much of Namibia, the canyon – which is actually a canyon within a canyon and contains rock that is around 1.8 billion years old – is a paradise for geologists.

The formation of the Fish River Canyon began around 500 million years ago with a fracture in the earth's crust, which was deepened by retreating glaciers about 200 million years later. Further tectonic movements and erosion created a second layer and some 50 million years ago the Fish River began to cut its way along a valley floor.

Archaeological evidence suggests there was human habitation here some 50,000 years ago. Stone Age sites have been found near river bends, as well as many more recent remains of pre-colonial herders' camps. German soldiers used the area around the Ai-Ais hot springs on the bed of the Fish River as a base during their war against the Namas in 1904.

There are several observation points on the rim from which to view the grandeur and watch the kaleidoscope of colours in the changing light. The canyon is surprisingly little visited and you may find yourself marvelling at the hypnotic panorama in solitary splendour.

The main viewpoint, which has picnic tables under thatch, is about 10km (6 miles) from the park gate at

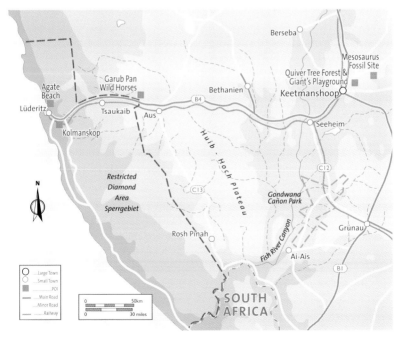

The Fish River snakes on its way through the awesome Fish River Canyon

Hobas. From here you get the classic view of the snaking river at Hell's Bend, a scene portrayed in so many photographs. About 3km (2 miles) to the right there's another good spot called Hiker's Viewpoint from which you get a different angle on the sheer immensity of the canyon. This is where hikers begin their steep descent on the arduous 85km (53 mile) Fish River Canyon Hiking Trail.

Fish River Canyon Trail

This challenging backpackers' hiking trail starts at the northernmost lookout point near Hobas and ends around 85km (53 miles) later at the Ai-Ais thermal hot springs resort in the south. A true wilderness trek, strictly for the very fit and experienced, it is a four- to five-day hike and everything has to be carried as there are no facilities of any kind along the route. The trail can be undertaken, by groups of at least three people, between 15 April and 15 September only and has to be booked well in advance. It is not possible to do day hikes in the canyon.

For hiking trail information and bookings contact Namibia Wildlife Resorts in Windhoek. Tel: (064) 285 7200. www.nwr.com.na

Gondwana Cañon Park

On the edge of the Fish River Canyon conservation area, this 1,120sq km (432sq mile) private nature reserve incorporates plateau mountains, dwarf shrub savannah and sweeping plains dotted with granite outcrops. The land was formerly used for sheep and cattle farming but is now the habitat of ostrich, mountain zebra, hartebeest, springbok and oryx.

Being only 20km (12 miles) from the Fish River Canyon, it is a convenient location for an overnight stay and there are four good accommodation establishments in the reserve (*see p162*).

KEETMANSHOOP

About 485km (301 miles) south of Windhoek, Keetmanshoop is where the main roads from Windhoek, South Africa and Lüderitz meet and is the administrative centre of the region. It's a clean and tidy town with wide streets, and while it doesn't have too many highlights, with its banks, supermarkets, petrol stations and pleasant hotels it's a good place to stock up and get organised before continuing on your journey.

Keetmanshoop ('Keetman's hope') was named after a rich industrialist, Johan Keetman, who gave 2,000 Reichmarks to a Rhenish Mission Society pastor to build a church in what was then a settlement of Nama people, who had trekked north from South Africa, called Swartmodder ('black mud'). The church was washed away in a freak flood in 1890 but was rebuilt on higher ground and now houses the museum (*see below*). Keetman himself never saw the town that bears his name.

There are several buildings dating from German colonial times, the most notable being the Kaiserliches Postamt (Imperial Post Office) dating from 1910, which faces onto an attractive garden square and is used by the tourist information office.

Keetmanshoop Museum

An oxwagon and a Nama hut stand in the colourful gardens planted with aloes and native species that surround the pretty stone church. Inside there are collections of old photographs and memorabilia of life in the town.
Sam Nujoma Drive. Tel: (063) 221 256. Open: Mon–Thur 7am–12.30pm & 1.30–4.30pm, Fri 7am–12.30pm & 1.30–4pm. Free admission but donations welcomed.

Quiver Tree Forest and Giant's Playground

Quiver trees (*Aloe dichotoma*), also known as *kokerboom* in Afrikaans, are tree-aloes that grow on steep, stony slopes across southern Namibia and the northern Cape in South Africa. They are usually found singly, which is why the large stand of about 250 of them 14km (9 miles) northeast of Keetmanshoop can be termed a 'forest'. These trees are estimated to be between 200 and 300 years old.

Quiver trees get their popular name from the San people who made quivers for their arrows from the hollow branches. With their pale bark and graphically shaped branches crowned by sprays of succulent leaves, they look almost prehistoric and quite spectacular against a deep blue southern sky. They flower in June and July with a mass of bright yellow blooms.

A National Heritage Site, the Quiver Tree Forest is on the privately owned Farm Gariganus, which charges a rather hefty fee to visit them. Also on the property, a maze of massive dolerite boulders – around 160 million years old – is piled, stacked and balanced in higgledy-piggledy formations as if bricks in a giant's playground, hence

the name. Walking among them makes you feel very small.

The Quiver Tree Forest is 14km (9 miles) northeast of Keetmanshoop. Signposted off the C17 north of Keetmanshoop. Tel: (063) 222 835.

Mesosaurus fossil site

If you continue driving along the gravel road past Giant's Playground you reach the less well-known balancing rock stacks and a grove of quiver trees at this site, where fossilised skeletons about 50cm (20in) long of *Mesosaurus tenuidens* are imprinted in the slate. This reptile lived about 260 million years ago in the vast shallow sea that once covered large parts of southern Africa.

42km (26 miles) northeast of Keetmanshoop. Open site.

Teetering rocks stack up in the Giant's Playground

A stand of the strange kokerboom tree aloes in the Quiver Tree Forest

AUS

Known mainly for its extremes of weather – very hot in summer, freezing in winter – and for being the site of a prisoner-of-war camp during World War I, the hilltown of Aus is easy to miss when driving along the main B4 road west from Keetmanshoop to Lüderitz. But do stop at **Aus Info**, a striking pink and white building perched above the Aus turn-off. A community-run project, it is arguably the best information centre in Namibia. With its well-designed, information-packed display boards, here you will learn about the town, its people and historic sites, the wild horses of the Namib and the extraordinary diversity of the flora.

More than 500 different plant species grow in the surrounding desert, about 60 of them endemic to Namibia,

and seven of those can be found only around Aus. There are insects and animals here, too, that are found nowhere else in the world. Being situated on the fringe of two rainfall areas and at the meeting point of three deserts makes this region a unique environment.

Run by the Aus Community Conservation Trust, Aus Info also has a café and restaurant serving light meals, a small crafts shop and a nursery growing quiver trees and succulents. *Aus Info. Tel: (063) 258 151. Open: 8am–5pm.*

Wild desert horses

Feral horses roam the plains at the foot of the Aus mountains. Garub Pan, their waterhole, is signed along the B4 about 20km (12 miles) west of Aus (*see above*).

Wild horses of the Namib

Wild horses, possibly the only wild desert-dwelling horses in the world, live on the barren Garub plains at the foot of the Aus Mountains in the southwestern reaches of the Namib-Naukluft National Park. They are not indigenous and how they got there originally has given rise to many theories and much speculation, but generations have successfully survived there for nigh on a century.

The most likely explanation is that they were victims of World War I. In early 1915, retreating German *Schutztruppe* with 2,000 horses were at Aus, closely followed by South African troops. There are reports from the time of 10,000 South African soldiers and 6,000 horses encamped at Garub, also of a daring raid by a German pilot dropping bombs on the camp and on 1,700 grazing cavalry horses. In the ensuing chaos it is quite possible that many horses fled and were not recaptured.

This may explain the origins of the initial group, but the diversity of characteristics in the feral horses of the Namib suggests they were joined by horses from a different source. A stud farm south of Aus, owned by Emil Kreplin, the first mayor of Lüderitz, may provide the answer.

Kreplin bred horses both for use in the diamond mines and for the very popular horse racing events held in the boomtown's heyday.

As the region was part of the diamond-rich *Sperrgebiet* ('forbidden area') and very strictly controlled, the horses were left to roam free. A borehole at Garub provided water, as it still does. In 1986, this part of the *Sperrgebiet* was declared no longer off-limits and was incorporated into the Namib-Naukluft National Park.

Now regarded as a breed in their own right, over the decades the horses adapted their feeding and drinking habits to the harsh conditions of life at the edge of the Namib Desert. They drink less frequently than domestic horses, despite the heat, and supplement their diet by eating their dry dung, which contains three times more fat and almost twice as much protein as the area's dry grass.

Their numbers fluctuate between around 90 and 150 according to the quantity and quality of the grazing. During dry conditions they roam over large distances, while after good rains they stay closer to the water trough, feeding at night and spending more time at play during the day.

The wild horses form breeding groups that are led by a mare, which decides all the group's activities, and are protected by one or two stallions, which keep the bachelor groups at bay. As the mares choose which stallion they will mate with, fights are rare.

The B4 road between Keetmanshoop and Lüderitz passes by their territory. A gravel track signed 'feral horses', *about 20km (12 miles) west of Aus, leads to the Garub Pan and the horses' drinking trough. You can watch them from a shelter there. The nearby Klein-Aus Vista lodge (see p162) has a special permit for excursions into the area. Guests can book late-afternoon game drives to visit them and see spectacular sunsets over the plains and surrounding mountains.*

Wild horses roam the desert plains near Aus, their origins a mystery

Desert rock near Aus blazes red in the setting sun

LÜDERITZ

Isolated between desert dunes, the diamond plains of the 26,000sq km (10,039sq mile) *Sperrgebiet* ('forbidden zone') and the pounding South Atlantic, windswept Lüderitz seems to be in a world of its own. Boasting fine German colonial architecture and houses painted in pretty pastel shades, it is a town of character.

A little history

The Portuguese navigator and explorer Bartolomeu Dias sailed into the bay in December 1487, before rounding the Cape of Good Hope in such bad weather that he named it Cabo Tormentosa (Cape of Storms). On his return journey to Lisbon the following year, he erected a *padrão* (stone cross) at what is now known as Diaz Point

on the Lüderitz Peninsula and which he called Angra Pequena (Small Cove). But Portugal made no claim to the land, considering it too desolate and forbidding.

Four centuries later, whalers, sealers, fishing boats and guano collectors filled the bay. In April 1833, Franz Adolf Lüderitz, a tobacco merchant from Bremen in Germany, landed at Angra Pequena with the intention of starting up a trading station. He sent his trader friend Heinrich Vogelsang into the interior as his agent to negotiate with a local Nama chief in Bethanie, Josef Frederiks, for some land.

Vogelsang purchased all the land within an 8km (5 mile) radius of Angra Pequena for £100 in gold coins and 200 rifles, then a swathe of the coast south to the Orange River for £500 and 60 rifles. Little did anyone realise that the area secreted one of the richest alluvial diamond fields in the world. The cash was never handed over. Instead, an amount considered the equivalent was given in traded goods.

The raising of the German flag at Angra Pequena, which was renamed Lüderitzbucht (Lüderitz Bay), marked the start of German colonial control of Namibia. Later, Franz Adolf Lüderitz bought all the land north to the Kunene River for £170. He had purchased the coast of what would soon become Deutsch-Südwest-Afrika (German South West Africa).

Diamond town

Used first as a supply base for the *Schutztruppe* (German colonial forces) during the 1904–7 German-Nama war, the town of Lüderitz developed and grew rich on the diamonds that were discovered nearby in 1908. Its attractive colonial architecture, clinging to the grey rocks above the bay, dates from this period. Decorative gables and friezes, bow and oriel windows, turrets, steep roofs and winding stairwells present an image that's unique in Africa.

After 1938, when more diamond fields had been discovered and the

An inviting beachside café at Diaz Point on the tip of the Lüderitz Peninsula

mining conglomerate decamped to Oranjemund down the coast close to Namibia's border with South Africa, the town went into decline. As if waking from a long sleep, today Lüderitz is sprouting new developments and attracting many more visitors, and there's a tangible sense of resurgence in the air.

Situated on the only rocky shoreline in Namibia, the town is surrounded by an indented coast, a jagged peninsula jutting out to sea (*see pp64–5*) and a scattering of barren islands where seabirds roost and breed. There are many coves, lagoons and beaches, although the icy Benguela Current does not encourage swimming. They can feel very bleak when the wind that buffets Lüderitz for much of the year is at its strongest, but are perfect for long lonely walks and a spot of beachcombing.

Agate beach

A long stretch of sheltered beach 8km (5 miles) north of town. Backed by wind-whipped dunes and the gneiss rocks of the *Sperrgebiet*, it is a favourite with locals at weekends. There are *braai* (barbecue) sites and picnic tables in the dunes, gulls, cormorants and long-legged waders in the shallows, while flamingos often gather in the small pond nearby.

Colourful houses in Berg Street date back to the diamond boomtown days

Lüderitz from the sea

Felsenkirche
(Church on the Rocks)

Perched atop a hill and visible from all over town, this German Evangelical Lutheran church, known by everyone as the Felsenkirche, was built in 1912 and has very fine stained-glass windows. In powerful jewel-like colours they were mainly paid for from donations by the diamond-rich local community, but the window behind the altar was given by Kaiser Wilhelm II. The architectural design of the church is interesting, as it is not in the preferred German neo-Gothic style of that period, but rather resembles the vertical-Gothic so popular in Victorian England.

NACOBTA

Namibia Community-Based Tourism Association (NACOBTA) is a non-profit membership organisation that assists communities in the previously neglected rural areas to generate income and employment through tourism. Established in 1995 with the goal of improving living standards among rural Namibians, it offers training in tourism, tour guiding and business skills, obtains funding for viable new ventures and provides marketing, lobbying and a booking and information service for the enterprises. The locally run activities, accommodation and arts and crafts enterprises give visitors the opportunity to be in contact with and gain insight into the many cultures that make up Namibia.
www.nacobta.com.na

Diamantberg. Open: Mon–Sat 5–6pm (summer); 4–5pm (winter). Donations welcomed.

Goerke Haus (Goerke House)

This 'diamond palace' built in 1909 by Hans Goerke, a former member of the *Schutztruppe* who joined the diamond rush, is the highlight of Lüderitz's Art Nouveau buildings. Built among the rocks of Diamantberg (Diamond Mountain) with panoramic views across the town and bay, Goerke House is full of colour and detail and furnished in the style of the era.

The hilltop Felsenkirche is a Lüderitz landmark

Built for his German bride Louise, whom Goerke married in 1910, no expense was spared in the construction and decoration of the house. He even managed to secure an electricity supply in 1911, by hooking up with the Kapps Hotel at the bottom of the hill. This was a time when champagne and beer were cheaper than water, which was shipped up from Cape Town. But perhaps Louise was less than impressed, because Goerke returned to Germany in 1912.

The house was sold several times over the following decades, each time for considerably less than the 70,000 Reichmarks it cost to build. At one time it was the residence of the local magistrate. Bought by Consolidated Diamond Mines (CDM) in 1981 to open as a museum, renovation and restoration began in 1983.

Although parts of the house have been modernised – it is used as a guesthouse for VIP visitors – the work has been done sensitively. Motifs and friezes have been restored and the new curtains are in patterns typical of the period.

The original Oregon pine flooring is still in place and some of the linoleum that once covered it appears on the floor in the study. Many of the light fittings are classic originals and the beautiful furniture has been chosen with care. Striking stained-glass windows, depicting pink flamingos on the lagoon, light the impressive carved wood staircase. The stained

Goerke House, built in the Art Nouveau style by a diamond magnate, is essential viewing

glass in the entrance hall is original, too. Full of atmosphere, it's an exciting house to explore.

Diamantberg St. Open: Mon–Fri 2–4pm, Sat & Sun 4–5pm. Closed: public holidays

---

DIAMOND BONANZA

It was an Owambo railway worker, Zacharias Lewala, who found the stone while clearing sand at Grasplatz siding near Lüderitz in April 1908. He handed it to his German foreman, August Stauch, who, finding it would scratch glass, posted a claim to the area and then announced that a diamond had been discovered.

So began the great diamond prospecting rush. Over 5 million carats were found between 1908 and the start of World War I in 1914. It is said that on moonlit nights so many crystals glittered across the desert gravel that they could be picked up by the handful.

---

and when in use as a VIP guesthouse. Admission charge.

Lüderitz Museum

The core of the exhibits here stems from a private collection of Friedrich Eberlanz, who arrived in Lüderitz in 1914 and opened the museum in 1961. Together with the cases of local flora and fauna, rocks, stones and an egg collection, there's an interesting section on the Bushmen and Namibia's indigenous people. Old photographs show the development of Lüderitz and give an idea of the mining lifestyle and entertainment, which included horse racing. There's a section on the diamond mining industry, too.

Diaz St. Tel: (063) 202 532. Open: Mon–Fri 3.30–5pm. Admission charge.

Lüderitz harbour

Schooner cruises

Weather permitting, the schooner *Sedina* departs under sail for Diaz Point and the African penguin colony on Halifax Island. The boat is often accompanied by Heavyside dolphins and you can also expect to see Cape fur seals and a host of birdlife.

Waterfront jetty. Tel: (063) 204 030. Departures daily at 8am, cruising time about two hours.

Shark Island

A causeway joins the erstwhile island and its lighthouse to the mainland. There are great sea views from the rocks where plaques commemorate some of the people who gave Lüderitz its history (but omit to mention the people who died here when the island was a notorious concentration camp).

Waterfront

A new development with shops and cafés alongside the harbour. It's a good place to stop for coffee or lunch and watch the activity of fishing trawlers and the small boats used by diamond-divers.

KOLMANSKOP

Once there were grand houses and gambling saloons in what is now a surreal ghost town abandoned to the desert sand. The first of the diamond-rush towns, Kolmanskop sits on a wind-ravaged hill about 13km (8 miles) inland from Lüderitz.

Settlement began in 1908, but its heyday was the 1920s when it was a thriving community boasting the latest commodities, including an ice-making plant, an early form of air-conditioning, electricity – coal was imported from Germany to fire the power plant – Namibia's first library and even a swimming pool.

Water was shipped in from Cape Town and each family received 20 litres (35 pints) and half a block of ice a day for free. A fully equipped hospital housed the first X-ray machine in southern Africa, its main use being to detect diamonds secreted by Owambo contract workers who lived in appalling conditions in sheds some distance away.

For entertainment there were champagne and cigar bars, an à la carte restaurant employing six chefs, two skittle alleys (one for women, one for men) and a concert hall staging lavish shows. Some of the main buildings have been restored, including the theatre and mine manager's house, which is furnished.

Kolmanskop's fascinating story is told on a guided tour, after which you are free to explore the abandoned buildings piled high with drifting sand. Don't miss the evocative old photographs in the restaurant or the information display boards in the Diamond Room.

Open: 8am–1pm, guided tours Mon–Sat 9.30am & 11am, Sun & public holidays 10am. Admission charge includes tour.

Sand is slowly devouring buildings at Kolmanskop, a diamond mining ghost town with an amazing history

Walk: Lüderitz town

Handsome colonial buildings dating from the early 20th century give central Lüderitz its distinctive character. A gentle walk through its streets reveals gables, turrets, towers and colourful façades.

Allow two hours, longer if you plan to see inside the Goerke House and Felsenkirche, which open in the afternoons. Approximate distance: 5km (3 miles).

Start at the waterfront complex on Hafen St. Pass the harbour gates and turn left into Bismarck St.

1 The fountain

The fountain celebrates the laying of a pipeline in 1969 bringing fresh water to Lüderitz. Previously, water had been supplied by a desalination plant and was a costly commodity.

To visit the small Lüderitz Museum (see p59), walk to the right on Diaz St. Otherwise continue up Bismarck St.

2 Old Railway Station

Bismarck Street is the main shopping and commercial thoroughfare. At the top of the street, the ornate Old Railway Station, dating from 1913, is a national monument.

Turn right on Nachtigal St, then left into Berg St.

3 Berg Street

Built between 1908 and 1911, colourful shop-houses line the street. Their owners included a baker, photographer and a supplier of curtains, carpets and saddles. The house at the corner, now called Grünewald, was built by August Stauch, the man who was handed the first diamond at Grasplatz and kicked off the frenzy (*see p59*). At the top, Kreplin House (1909) was the home of diamond magnate Emil Kreplin, the town's first mayor.

Berg St becomes Kirche St and leads steeply up to the church.

4 Felsenkirche and Goerke Haus

The landmark church (*see p57*) has magnificent stained-glass windows and panoramic views across the town and bay. Go back down the hill and turn right into Diamantberg Street to see the fabulous Art Nouveau-style Goerke House (*see p58*).

Walk downhill along Zeppelin St, turning right at the T-junction. Cross Bismarck St and the old railway bridge. Turn left into Baie St. Mabel St is on the right.

5 Mabel Street

Privately owned and beautifully cared
for, all the impressive-looking houses on
the right (south) side of Mabel Street
were built for the Imperial German
Railway Commissioner's office in 1908.
Return to Baie St, turn right.

6 Diaz Tiles

A Portuguese ceramic tile picture
depicting the landing of Bartolomeu
Dias in 1488 is fronted by a small
garden and a ship's anchor. Portuguese
residents of Namibia donated the
picture to the town in 1988 to celebrate
the 500th anniversary of the explorer's
landing. Across the road, an Art
Nouveau sunray design denotes Kapps

Hotel and the ballroom that hosted
galas, concerts and glittering events
during the boom years.
Turn right up Ring St.

7 Turnhalle and Lesehalle

The beautiful green-domed Lesehalle
houses the evocative public library, and
the lovely pink and ochre Turnhalle,
opened in 1918, is used for functions.
*Follow Schinz St round to the
Kaiserliches Postamt (Imperial Post
Office), a national monument now
occupied by Namibia Wildlife Resorts.
A right turn brings you back to the Old
Railway Station and into Bismarck St. At
the bottom of Bismarck St, turn right to
return to the waterfront.*

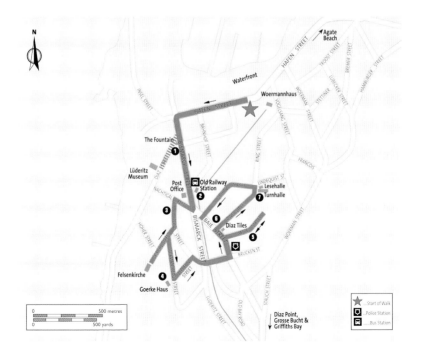

Drive: Lüderitz Peninsula

A rocky desert surrounded by the ocean on three sides, the peninsula lies to the southwest of town. It is partly in the restricted diamond area of the Sperrgebiet and, although the moonscape of dark gneiss rocks can at times look inhospitable, there are numerous sandy beaches, a variety of birds and plants and even some wildlife sightings.

In good weather this is a pleasant half-day tour, driving some 65km (40 miles) on gravel roads.

Follow Lüderitz St out of town. Just after the yellow-painted, fort-like building (the prison), make a right turn at the sign for Diaz Point.

1 Second lagoon

Driving through a rock and dune landscape, stop at the lagoon to check for flamingos. A map there details the Diamond Coast Recreational Area.
Continue along the road until the sign for Griffiths Bay. Turn right onto D734.

2 Griffiths Bay

Amid low rocky hills, desert-adapted plants drape over boulders and succulents form cushions in the roadside sand and gravel. Kelp gulls gather at the glacial, wind-whipped water's edge and there's a good view across to Lüderitz from the beach.
Return to the main road (D701), turn right, and after a short distance go left at the sign for Grosse Bucht (D733).

3 Grosse Bucht

Living up to its name ('big bay'), the sweeping beach of grey, dark sand has dunes covered with succulent plants in striking shades of maroon and green. Long, white-crested waves roll onto the kelp-strewn beach and flamingos trawl in the foam. Watch out for springbok as you drive on the winding road there.
Return to the main road. Turn left for Diaz Point.

4 Shearwater Bay

There are shimmering blue saltpans on both sides of the road as you head through a parched and bleached landscape, and a switchback ride amid bitter black rock reveals a wide expanse

The cross of Diaz Point

of beach with a red-and-white-striped lighthouse on the far point.
Continue on to Diaz Point.

5 Diaz Point

There's a terrific little café on the beach at Diaz Point, just what you need after you've crossed the wooden bridge and climbed the steep steps up to the cross on the windy headland. The cross is a replica of the *padrão* planted by Bartolomeu Dias in 1488 when he named the point Angra Pequena.

Head back the way you came, but look for a turn on the right, signed Grosse Bucht. When you see the ruins of an old guano factory across the bay, take the right fork.

6 Halifax Island

A small beach is the lookout point for Halifax Island. Waves pound over the rocks that are home to the third-largest colony of African penguins to be found in Namibia.
Return to the D701 and Lüderitz.

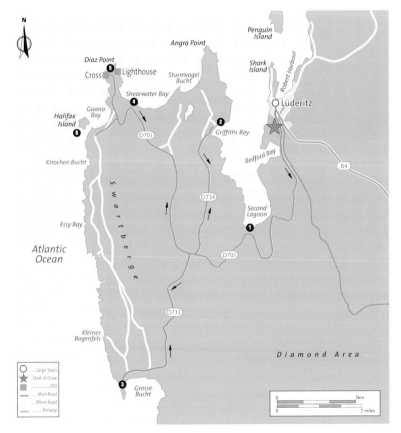

The Namib Desert

The desert that gave the country its name extends all the way down Namibia's coastline for over 1,600km (994 miles) and spreads inland for up to 140km (87 miles) east to west. With petrified dunes lying beneath the ever-moving sands, the Namib is held to be the world's oldest desert. It supports some extraordinary flora and fauna, like the Welwitschia *and the oryx, often known as 'gemsbok', an antelope that can survive for months without drinking.*

Among its many and varied landscapes are rocky mountains, gravel plains, gorges, canyons, clay pans, ephemeral rivers, the mysterious Skeleton Coast and the most spectacular sea of sand dunes in the world.

At the coast, affected by the cold Benguela Current in the South Atlantic, it is a cool desert, dry, windy and often blanketed by the fog that brings moisture and life to desert-adapted plants and insects. But in the mountains, pans and dunes temperatures can top 40°C (104°F) in summer and drop to freezing on winter nights.

The Namib-Naukluft National Park lies at the heart of the Namib. One of the largest conservation areas on the African continent, with a surface area of 49,768sq km (19,216sq miles), it is bigger than Switzerland. Ostrich, springbok and oryx roam the plains, Hartmann's mountain zebra, klipspringer and baboons frequent canyons.

The highlight, however, is the great sand sea of towering, star-shaped dunes at Sossusvlei and the surreal clay pan of Dead Vlei, where the colours and the views are one of life's take-your-breath-away experiences.

DUNES

The sand dunes of the Namib Desert come in many shapes and forms. They vary in colour and size but all are composed of grains of quartz with the addition of small quantities of heavy minerals.

A dune rests on a 'base' of coarse, deeply rippled sand where wind-blown detritus of plant and animal material feeds the insects and life at the bottom of the food chain. The 'dune slope' above the base, at an angle of 14° from horizontal, often supports some vegetation. Sand is constantly cascading down the 'slip face' near the crest of the dune, which lies at an angle of 32°–34° above the horizontal.

Transverse, parabolic, star, barchan and parallel linear dunes are all found in the Namib.

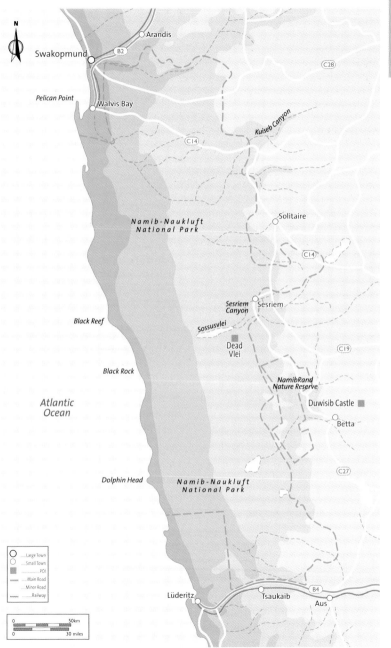

The Namib Desert

Dunes in the Namib Desert

Transverse dunes can be seen close to the coast and south of Walvis Bay. Their axes lie perpendicular to the strong winds blowing from the south and they have massive slip faces.

The combination of southerly and easterly winds in the central Namib has formed parallel, linear dunes. Around 100m (328ft) high and standing about 1km (⅔ mile) apart, they have slip faces that reverse direction depending on whether the wind is blowing from the south (between September and April) or east. Multi-armed star dunes top the linear ridges when they are buffeted by wind from all sides.

All sand is on the move to some extent, but the fastest, most mobile dunes are the crescent-shaped barchans. Created by wind blowing strongly from a single direction, they tend to be low and with long outstretched arms they march forward covering everything in their wake. Some of the finest examples of barchan dunes are found around Lüderitz, especially at the ghost mining town of Kolmanskop (*see pp60–61*) where the wind-whipped sand seems to be devouring the abandoned buildings.

Parabolic, or multi-cyclic, dunes are a feature of Sossusvlei. There, winds of almost equal strength blow from different directions during the year.

DUWISIB CASTLE

On the edge of the desert and surrounded by rolling hills, this extraordinary red sandstone castle, complete with turrets and castellated walls, was built by Hansheinrich von Wolf from Saxony, a captain in the *Schutztruppe*, for his American heiress wife Jayta.

Builders and stonemasons from Italy and carpenters from Germany and Sweden were employed to build Duwisib Castle, which was completed in 1909. All the furnishings were brought from Germany – transported first by rail from the port at Lüderitz to Aus, from where it took 20 journeys by ox-wagon to deliver it all. Von Wolf bought up large tracts of farming land, bred fine horses and imported Hereford bulls from England.

Although sparsely furnished, the castle houses some interesting antiques in the baronial rooms and the castle is worth visiting if only for the sheer

NAMIBIAN WINE

Wine is being produced at the farm Neuras on the eastern fringe of the Naukluft Mountains, where Alan Walkden-Davis planted the first vines in 1997. He has under a hectare (less than two acres) under cultivation, with about 1,100 vines of the Shiraz variety and 200 of Merlot, and a good harvest results in around 1,000 bottles of wine.

Namibia's second winery is at Omaruru, northeast of Windhoek. Helmut Kluge at Kristall Kellerei produces two red wines, Ruby Cabernet and Cabernet Sauvignon, a white wine, Colmard, as well as a brandy and Schnapps produced from prickly pears and lemons.

incongruity of it all. Venerable jacaranda trees fill the courtyard garden and there's a cosy café in the grounds.
Open: 8am–1pm & 2–5pm.
Admission charge.

Duwisib Castle, a desert fantasy with an extraordinary story

FAIRY CIRCLES

Circular patches of completely bare sandy soil, known as 'fairy circles', are a feature of the grassland landscape around Sossusvlei and the fringes of the Namib Desert. Although why they happen remains a mystery, there are several theories about their origin: poisonous *Euphorbia damarana* bushes once grew there; they are the sites of old ostrich nests; termites have killed the grasses; there is a fungus in the ground that prohibits growth. Then there's the story that they are UFO landing sites. Despite years of study, scientists have been unable to explain the phenomenon. Perhaps the fairies really have been busy...

NAMIB-NAUKLUFT NATIONAL PARK

An amalgamation of the Namib Desert Park (proclaimed in 1907), the Naukluft Mountain Zebra Park (created in 1966) and two previously forbidden sections of the Diamond Area, the vast Namib-Naukluft National Park stretches from the Swakop River in the north down to the main road to Lüderitz in the south.

Within its boundaries are lagoons and arid gravel plains, high plateaus and deep sculpted canyons, wildlife and wilderness, flat white pans and soaring apricot dunes.

Dry riverbeds head westwards. Often referred to as 'linear oases', their underground water supply supports countless trees and shrubs, bringing splashes of green to a background of soft sand and offering shade and food to animals, birds and insects. *Inselbergs* ('isolated mountains') of granite, marble or schist rise up from wide plains, their height accentuated by the flatness of their surroundings. They capture moisture from mist and fog rolling far inland from the coast, and when rain falls it runs off the rock into crevices where plants and myriad creatures thrive.

The Namib Desert Park section of the national park includes the wild and lonely Kuiseb Canyon with its maze of deep ravines and the flat gravel welwitschia plains and 'moonscape' near Swakopmund (*see p78*). Here the curvature of the earth can be clearly seen, and as you stand alongside strange plants hundreds of years old there's a sense of being the only person inhabiting the world.

The rugged Naukluft Park region, a mountainous area accessible only on foot or horseback, has deep gorges with perennial streams and supports a wide variety of plants, trees, birds and animals. With three designated trails, this is excellent country for experienced hikers. It was originally formed as a sanctuary for Hartmann's mountain zebra (*Equus zebra hartmannae*), which were competing with livestock for grazing on farms. Found only in Namibia and southern Angola, they are slightly taller and lack the brown shadow markings of the Burchell's zebra (*Equus burchelli*) that inhabit the plains.

However, it is the spectacular sand dunes around Sossusvlei that draw most visitors to the Namib-Naukluft National Park.

Dead Vlei

Even more spectacular than the *vlei* (pan) of Sossusvlei, nearby Dead Vlei is a ghostly white pan where the dark outlines of ancient camelthorn trees, between 500 and 600 years old, rise from the white clay against a backdrop of soaring terracotta dunes and a cloudless, deep blue sky.

It's a dramatic, surreally beautiful sight, involving a 2km (1¹/₄ mile) walk from the car park (which is a couple of minutes' drive from the Sossusvlei car park) across sand and a low dune ridge, and you really shouldn't miss it. If you are lucky, a lone oryx will appear and wend its way across the sand. Then the picture-postcard image will be complete.

Kuiseb Canyon

In a maze of harsh bare rock and deep ravines at the edge of the Park, the Kuiseb Canyon forms a barrier against the southern desert dunes.

The steep pass through it is a zigzagging, heart-stopping drive among powerful rock formations of fascinating shapes, colours and textures. There are impressive lookout points above the bridge that crosses the usually dry riverbed.

It was here that two German geologists, Henno Martin and Hermann Korn, hid for over two years to avoid internment during World War II. If you haven't already read *The Sheltering Desert*, the book that tells the story of their time there, you'll want to read it when you've seen the inhospitable environment that they somehow managed to survive in. Their first shelter under a big overhanging rock can still be visited.

Sesriem Canyon

A slash in the earth about 1km (²/₃ mile) long, this narrow gorge carved by the Tsauchab River some 15 million years

Dead Vlei, a surreal white clay pan ringed by high dunes of red sand

Walking through the Sesriem Canyon

ago is up to 40m (130ft) deep in places. It gets its name from the days when early pioneers tied together six lengths of oxhide thongs (*ses riems* in Afrikaans) to lower their buckets and draw water from the pools at its base. Unless there has been heavy rain, you can walk along the sandy floor and look up at the intriguingly patterned layers of rock.

The canyon could be visited when you have completed your visit to Sossusvlei and Dead Vlei. It is about 4km (2½ miles) south of the permit office at the Sesriem gate, reached along a rock-strewn gravel road.

NAMIBRAND NATURE RESERVE

Bordering on the Namib-Naukluft National Park south of Sesriem, at nearly 180,000ha (444,780 acres) the NamibRand is one of the largest private reserves in southern Africa. Formerly a collection of farms, it has some spectacular desert scenery, including tall red dunes, tree-filled valleys, vast stretches of grass savannah and high mountains. Among the animals roaming the landscape are springbok, oryx, ostrich, red hartebeest, zebra, spotted hyena, kudu and the much more elusive leopard, while 120 bird species have been recorded. Several upmarket lodges conveniently located for visiting Sossusvlei are located in the reserve (*see pp164–5*).

SOLITAIRE

Between Sesriem and the Kuiseb Canyon there's a quirky little place called Solitaire. This is the desert's 'Wild West' one-horse town, but so offbeat and idiosyncratic it has been used as a film location.

Behind the filling station, the big news of the day is chalked up on a board outside the open-all-hours General Dealer, which stocks pretty much everything, including quite a range of books and crafts, and is famed for its home-baked apple crumble.

The lively Solitaire Desert Festival happens here every December and includes music by local and South African bands, spit-roasted meats and quad bike racing.

About 70km (43 miles) south of the Kuiseb Canyon and 75km (47 miles) north of Sesriem.

Cacti in bloom at Solitaire

Sossusvlei

Monumental dunes stretch to the horizon like an ocean of sand mountains. Patterned by light and shadow, their colours sweep from pale pink and apricot through red, gold and purple in the ever-changing light of day. It's little wonder that Sossusvlei is one of Namibia's highlight destinations.

Entrance to the Sossusvlei valley is at Sesriem where the gates open daily at sunrise and close at sunset. You pay for your entrance permit there and can stock up on water, snacks and fuel.

Then it's an unforgettable 65km (40 mile) drive along an asphalt road lined with dunes that rise up to 375m (1,230ft) from base to peak, until you reach the 2WD car park, beyond which a saloon car cannot go. There are shuttle services onwards, or you can walk the final 5km (3 miles), but 4WD vehicles can continue on through the soft sand to the parking area alongside the *vlei* itself.

Here the cracked, grey-white surface of the pan is surrounded by trees, bush and high dunes. Birds sing, an ostrich or two may pad into view, and you are left to imagine how this dry valley bed looks on the rare occasions when heavy rains in the interior of the country bring the ephemeral Tsauchab River this far down and the flooded pan is covered with water and strutting flamingos. Once upon a time the Tsauchab flowed from the Great Escarpment to the Atlantic Ocean, until the dunes stopped it in its tracks some 60,000 years ago.

The dune experience: the road to Sossusvlei

The dunes are dynamic, their sinuous shapes and contours constantly shifting with the wind. Snaking, razor-sharp edges, where the slip face and windward sides of the dune meet, separate orange-red sand and near-black shade into pyramid-like sculptures.

The best time to experience them is in the early-morning light, both for the intensity of the colours and the fact that it's the coolest part of the day. Late afternoon is also a special time, but remember that the park gates close at sunset and that Sossusvlei is about an hour's drive from the gate at Sesriem.

At the start of the road to the *vlei*, parched grass and yellow sand sweep to the feet of distant red dunes. There may be sightings of large birds like the cory bustard as well as grazing springbok, a jackal in search of sustenance and ostriches trotting off on urgent business. Then for the last 30km (19 miles) the dunes are like ribs on both sides of the valley floor that you are driving along, swirling like whipped ice cream in myriad shapes and colours. Even the mirages on the road are pink.

Dune 45 (45km/28 miles from the gate) is a favourite stopping place and has its own parking area under the shade of acacia trees. After the long climb to the peak, when every step forward seems to result in two steps back, you'll be rewarded by a sweeping vista of wave upon wave of 'dune sea'.

If you have an additional day in the region, then an early morning balloon flight is an expensive but truly unforgettable experience. You are collected from your lodge before dawn and driven to the take-off site. To drift over the desert as the sun rises is magical, and a champagne breakfast is served when you land.

The great white *vlei* (pan) of Sossusvlei

Life in the desert

An extraordinary collection of plants, animals and insects inhabits Namibia's desert landscapes. They have all adapted to the arid conditions in their own way. Plants produce seeds that lie dormant for decades, shrubs tend to be low and slow growing, trees have either very narrow or fleshy leaves, animals may have a low metabolic rate and lizards 'dive' to retreat beneath the sand. The 'fog-basking' beetle (*Onymacris unguicularis*) does handstands, tipping its bottom upwards to catch a drop of fog dew, which then rolls down into its mouth. Ground squirrels turn their backs to the sun and use their tails as umbrellas during the heat of the day.

Animals
The African oryx (*Oryx gazella*) is the archetypal desert antelope. It can survive for very long periods without water and endure extremes of temperature thanks to a network of blood vessels that cools the blood in the nasal sinuses before it reaches the brain. Oryx are often seen on high sand dunes, which they climb to reach cooling breezes.

Endemic to the Namib Desert, the tiny (8cm/3in) blind burrower Grant's golden mole (*Eremitalpa granti*) has

strong shoulders for digging into termite nests and can cover 2km (over a mile) a night as it 'swims' through soft sand in search of sustenance.

Plants
The strangest plant must be the welwitschia (*Welwitschia mirabilis*). Endemic to a narrow coastal strip of the gravel Namib Desert, it grows in isolated communities and lives for hundreds of years.

A cone-bearing species with separate male and female plants, the welwitschia only ever produces two leaves, which can grow to 155m (509ft) long. Broad, leathery and

Animals seek the shade of desert trees in the heat of the day

The oryx can survive with very little water

strap-shaped, they lie on the ground and get shredded by the wind into a tangled mass of ribbons. Its taproot digs down 3m (10ft) and its leaves absorb moisture from overnight fogs. The winged seeds have an inhibitor that prevents germination until conditions are favourable for growth.

Often called 'living stones', lithops resemble the pebbles and stones that surround them, even mimicking their colours. Perfect camouflage for their succulent leaves.

A tangled thicket of vicious thorns, the !nara melon (*Acanthosicyos horrida*) is a Namib Desert endemic that has no leaves at all. Even its watery fruit is covered in thorns, but that doesn't deter oryx and other animals from eating it.

Trees

The prehistoric-looking quiver tree or *kokerboom* (*Aloe dichotoma*) grows on steep rocky slopes. It stores water in its fibrous trunk and branches and in its crown of thick succulent leaves, while a heavy waxy coating on exposed surfaces reduces water loss through transpiration.

The secret of the camelthorn (*Acacia erioloba*) is its root system. The taproot can penetrate to depths of 40m (130ft), lateral roots near the surface absorb light rain and mist and it even grows additional roots from the trunk when windblown sand piles up around it. Although the camelthorn grows everywhere in Namibia, it thrives in the desert, where its bright green foliage provides welcome shade and its thousands of seedpods are fodder for both farm and wild animals. Sociable weaver birds love to build their giant nests in its branches.

Swakopmund and the coast

Namibia's long coastline stretches 1,628km (1,012 miles) between its borders with Angola and South Africa, yet very little of it is inhabited. As well as the great impenetrable barrier of the Namib Desert dunes, there are some 500km (300 miles) of the wild Skeleton Coast to the north, while in the far south it's diamond country, mostly off-limits to visitors except for the appealing old town of Lüderitz (see p54).

Relaxed Swakopmund mixes old-world charm with fast-paced activities that have given the town the title 'Namibia's adventure capital'. Home to about 33,000 people, it is such a popular holiday and tourist destination that its population often more than doubles. High dunes back the road south to the deepwater port of Walvis Bay, famed for its birdlife and dolphins. Inland, ancient welwitschia plants dot the gravel plains of the Namib Desert.

Along the coast to the north are long stretches of sand, deserted for most of the year but packed in high season with holidaying Namibians, who set up their tents and *braais* (barbecues) to enjoy a Christmas break at the beach. From there on, it's angler's heaven.

The National West Coast Recreation Area incorporates isolated fishing communities and the popular holiday and retirement resort of Henties Bay. Further north, the sight of thousands of Cape fur seals at Cape Cross attracts

many visitors to their beach. The Portuguese explorer Diogo Cão, the first European to set foot on Namibian soil, erected a cross when he landed there in 1486.

Swakopmund's aptly named Palm Beach

SWAKOPMUND

With its palm trees and flower-filled public gardens, surf-washed beaches and fish restaurants, Swakopmund has the relaxed air of a seaside town. Elegant colonial German architecture mixes with low-rise modern buildings to line wide streets. A plethora of curio and gift shops tells of a population swelled by visitors. Finding accommodation here becomes difficult over the high summer holidays of December and January when there's an exodus to the coast to escape the heat in the interior of the country.

Between the desert and the sea, Swakopmund strikes an unexpected and individual pose. Although there was no bay, shelter or landing site, it

began life as a German harbour town, the first settlers arriving in small boats in 1893. With the port at Walvis Bay under British control, Germany needed its own harbour and transport connections into the interior.

Ox wagons were the only form of transport, but feeding and watering large numbers of oxen as they travelled great distances through the desert was a near impossible task. A disastrous outbreak of *rinderpest* (cattle plague) in 1897 proved the final straw and work began on the laying of a narrow-gauge railway line in September of that year. In June 1902, the first train travelled from Swakopmund to Windhoek, a distance of 382km (237 miles).

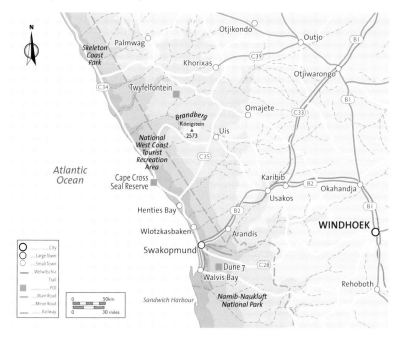

With the workforce, equipment and buildings required for the construction of both the harbour and the railway, and another privately built railway from the copper mine in Tsumeb in 1903–6, the settlement at Swakopmund grew quickly. In the first 14 years of the 20th century some very fine architecture graced the streets of the burgeoning new town. But in the aftermath of World War I, when South Africa took over the country's administration and developed Walvis Bay (33km/20 miles away) as the major port and business centre, Swakopmund lost its importance and went into decline.

After languishing in obscurity for years, the opening of an asphalt road from Windhoek in 1967, which drastically reduced the journey time to the coast, gave the town new life and it soon developed into a popular holiday haven and resort. Today, Swakop (as locals lovingly call it) is experiencing a building boom, with sea-view homes close to town, expanding suburbs and extensive new developments at Long Beach on the road south to Walvis Bay.

Hohenzollern House

German influences

Street names may have changed – Kaiser Wilhelm St has become Sam Nujoma Avenue, for example – but the German influence remains strong. With its immaculately restored colonial architecture, Swakopmund has often been called Klein Hamburg (Little Hamburg) and there's no shortage of apple strudel and Black Forest cake in the continental-style cafés and bakeries. Restaurants and bars serve beers brewed in the traditional German manner.

Eleven colonial buildings have been declared national monuments, including the old prison, which looks more like a grand Bavarian house displaced from a country estate. Among the highlights are **Woermann House** (*see p84*) and the **Hohenzollern House**, adorned with flowers and cupids, lions on the pediments, and topped by a statue of a kneeling Atlas with the world on his shoulders. Designed in the *Jugendstil* (Art Nouveau) style and built between 1904 and 1906 as a hotel, it is now an apartment building.

Imperial Germany's attempts to build a viable harbour were thwarted by ocean currents and the shifting sand that soon silted up the artificial basin formed by a breakwater mole, a massive engineering project that had cost 2.5 million Reichmarks to build. Jutting out to sea and lined with restaurants and cafés, today the Mole is one of Swakop's most popular meeting places. It forms a stone arm that shelters a sandy beach lined with tall palm trees, aptly named Palm Beach, and backed by gardens and a children's playground.

If you walk north along the seafront, past the Olympic-size municipal swimming pool with heated water, saunas and water slide, take a look at two striking colonial buildings on Ludwig Koch St. **Vierkantvilla** was prefabricated in Germany and shipped out to Swakopmund during the building of the Mole. The double-storey **Kabelmesse** was used by the Eastern and South Africa Telegraph Company that laid the undersea cable from Europe to Cape Town.

Set back from Palm Beach, the early 20th-century red-and-white-striped lighthouse is a distinctive landmark. It towers as a backdrop to the impressive Kaiserliches Bezirksgericht (Imperial District Court), now the president's summer holiday residence, which looks out over spacious public gardens and a big crafts market.

The town's position on the edge of the Namib Desert has spawned myriad adventure activities. From quad biking and sand boarding in the nearby dunes to skydiving, ballooning, paintball and rock climbing, there's plenty to excite the adrenalin junkie, while scenic flights in light aircraft are a thrilling way to experience the vastness and beauty of the desert and desolate Skeleton Coast.

Kristall Galerie

If you are planning to be in Swakopmund over a weekend, be aware that although some shops open on Sunday, the majority close from 1pm on Saturday until Monday morning and many restaurants do not open on Sunday night.

Kristall Galerie

Behind a very modern exterior lies a gallery housing the largest-known crystal cluster in the world, weighing 14,100kg (31,085lb) and estimated to be 520 million years old. It is surrounded by impressive displays of gemstones and you get to walk through a twist-and-turn tunnel replica of the original Otjua Tourmaline Mine where the giant crystal was found. Naturally there are some serious shopping opportunities, too.

Corner Tobias Hainyeko St & Theo-Ben Gurirab Ave. Tel: (064) 406 080. www.kristallgalerie.com. Open: Mon–Sat 9am–5pm. Admission charge.

National Marine Aquarium

Suitably sited along the beachfront, the highlight of the small aquarium is the glass walk-through tunnel in an oval-shaped transparent tank that contains a variety of fish found in coastal waters, including sharks, rays, steenbras, kabeljou and galjoen. Although mainly depicting marine life on an inshore reef, there are dry displays showing birds that breed along the Namibian coastline and explanations of the Benguela Current system. Children enjoy the touch pools, where the contents can be picked up and handled.

Feeding happens daily at 3pm, with feeding by divers taking place on Tuesday and weekends at 3pm.
Strand South St. Tel: (064) 410 1184. Open: Tue–Sat 10am–4pm, Sun 11am–5pm. Admission charge.

Otavi Bahnhof (Otavi Railway Station)

Next to the Sam Cohen Library (*see p84*), the restored Otavi Railway Station was built in 1906 to service the 60cm (23¹/₂in) narrow-gauge railway line constructed by the Otavi Mine and Railway Company (OMEG) to transport copper ore from Tsumeb in the north to the coast. Covering 567km (352 miles), the Otavi Railway Line was the longest narrow-gauge line in the world at that time.

The former goods shed now serves as a guesthouse. There's a small botanical garden with plants from the Namib Desert nearby.
Corner Sam Nujoma Ave & Windhoeker St. Tel: (064) 402 695. www.swakopmund-museum.org.na. Open: Mon–Fri 8am–1pm & 3–5pm, Sat 10am–noon. Free admission.

Swakopmund's fancifully ornate old Railway Station is now a hotel and entertainment complex

Sam Cohen Library and Museum

Some 8,000 volumes of a superb Africana collection are housed in the Sam Cohen Library, together with a unique archive of newspapers from 1898 to the present day and a large collection of historic photographs, maps and documents. For anyone interested in the local history, it's a fascinating place to browse.
Corner of Sam Nujoma Ave & Windhoeker St. Open: 10am–1pm & 2–5pm.

Swakopmund Museum

Spanning the plants and animals of the surrounding Namib Desert, numerous minerals found in Namibia and exhibits about nearby uranium mines, archaeology that sheds light on prehistory, information on the various ethnic peoples and a big section on the German colonial period, the country's largest privately run museum is an informative place to visit. It is housed in the old Imperial Customs House by the Mole and was founded in 1951 by a dentist, Dr Alfons Weber. His dental practice has been re-created (you'll be glad times have changed), and pioneer transport is represented by an original ox-wagon, with the carriage of the last German governor on display as a contrast.
Strand St, near the lighthouse.
Tel: (064) 402 046.
www.swakopmund-museum.org.na.
Open: 10am–1pm & 2–5pm.
Admission charge.

Woermann House

Dating from 1905, Woermann House is a handsome half-timbered building painted in shades of sand and ochre that now houses the public library and the Swakopmund Arts Association Gallery. Built for the Damara and Namaqua Trading Company and sold in 1909 to Woermann Brock & Co, the house was both business premises and a home but also welcomed visitors, from Prince Albrecht of Prussia to the farmers who came into town by ox-wagon to shop. The tower behind it was used as a lookout to watch for shipping activities in the bay – a flag would be hoisted whenever a ship of the Woermann Line was sighted – and for ox-wagons approaching from the desert. Don't miss the lovely courtyard at the back.
Bismarck St. Art gallery open: Mon–Fri 10am–noon & 3–5pm, Sat 10am–noon.

AROUND SWAKOPMUND
Cape Cross Seal Reserve

Cape Cross is home to a huge colony of Cape fur seals (*Arctocephalus pusillus pusillus*). Numbering between 80,000 and over 200,000 in the November–December breeding season, they are an amazing sight, draped over rocks, crashed out on the beach, surfing in the waves, basking in the sunshine, barking and snapping at intrusive neighbours and snoozing with a smile on their faces. The noise level is high as the young bleat like sheep and their elders honk and bark. The smell is

CAPE FUR SEALS

Although found along the coast from southern Angola down to South Africa, the biggest colony of Cape fur seals (*Arctocephalus pusillus pusillus*) on the mainland is at Cape Cross. Adult males (bulls) spend their time at sea, only coming ashore for the breeding season when they can weigh in at a massive 350kg (772lb). Each bull will have a harem of five to twenty-five females (cows) who give birth to a single pup. Mating occurs within a week of birthing, but the fertilised egg stays dormant for about 12 weeks before starting to develop as a foetus. Pups are usually born in November and December, weigh 4.5–7kg (10–15lb) and have black pelts.

pretty powerful, too, but can almost be forgotten as you become immersed in watching their antics.

The massive bulls usually arrive in October to stake out their territories, leaving after the females have given birth and they have mated, sometime in December. They return to sea to replenish the body fat lost while defending their territories.

About a week after the birth of her pup, the cow goes to sea to feed. When she returns she barks until she is reunited with her bleating pup. Many pups die fairly soon after birth, squashed by the huge weight and mass of the adult seals or eaten by the jackals and brown hyena that also inhabit the colony. The birthing period can therefore be a distressing time to visit and the stench is overwhelming, so if you are in Swakopmund towards the end of the year, it may be preferable to see seals on a boat trip from Walvis Bay.

The surviving young seals remain in the colony and continue suckling for about ten months.

Cape Cross is also the site of a *padrão* (limestone cross) erected by the Portuguese mariner and explorer Diogo Cão in 1486 when he landed there on his second African expedition in search of a trade route to the East. He was the first known European to set foot on Namibian soil, and the first to reach so far down the African coast. The cross was discovered in 1893 by a German surveying group and is now in the Deutsches Technikmuseum (German Science Museum) in Berlin.

It was first replaced with a wooden double cross and then in 1895, at the command of Kaiser Wilhelm II, by a carved stone cross. This depicted the Kaiser's crest and was placed 15m (49ft) southeast of the wooden one. In 1980, the National Monuments Council commissioned an exact replica of the Diogo Cão *padrão* to be carved from Namibian dolerite and erected on the spot where the original was found, which is why you'll find two crosses marking the landing site.

Cape Cross is along a salt road, which gets very slippery when wet. It is much used and well maintained, but care is needed as heavy early-morning mists can affect the surface. It is not advisable to drive this route after rain.

Cape Cross is 120km (75 miles) north of Swakopmund. Open: 10am–5pm. Admission charge.

Walk: Historic Swakopmund

With a palm-tree lined promenade skirting the beaches and a grid system of streets wide enough to turn an ox-wagon, the compact centre of Swakopmund is easy to walk around.

The highlights of this route are some beautifully preserved examples of colonial German architecture, but as there are innumerable shops to catch your eye and plenty of cafés to tempt you along the way, allow several hours to complete this 2.5km (1½ mile) stroll.

Starting at the Namib-i information centre on the corner of Hendrik Witbooi St, walk east on Sam Nujoma Ave then turn left on Otavi St.

1 Deutsche Evangelische Lutherische Kirche (German Evangelical Lutheran Church)

Consecrated in 1912, this impressive neo-Baroque church has a dome ceiling and colourful stained-glass windows. *Continue to the end of Otavi St where, on Theo-Ben Gurirab Ave, you will be facing the former railway station.*

2 Swakopmund Hotel and Entertainment Centre (Old Railway Station)

Preserved as a national monument and now housing a hotel and leisure complex, the old railway station, constructed in 1901–2, is a magnificent, fairytale-like building with a central tower and ornate façade. Take a look at the evocative photographs in the hotel and restaurant.

Continue west on Theo-Ben Gurirab Ave, passing brightly coloured apartments on the left. The striking entrance to the Kristall Galerie is on the corner of Tobias Hainyeko St.

3 Kristall Galerie

(*See p82.*)
Walk south on Tobias Hainyeko St, crossing to admire the painted façade of the gabled Altes Amtsgericht (Old Magistrate's Court), dated 1906, and turn right into a long amphitheatre of public gardens with a big crafts market down the centre.

4 Kaiserliches Bezirksgericht (State House)

Overlooking the gardens, this fort-like building, painted in khaki, green and white, the former District Court, is the summer residence of Namibia's president. The red-and-white-striped lighthouse towers in the gardens behind it.
Continue towards the sea, passing the lighthouse on your right.

5 Swakopmund Museum and the Mole

(*See p81 & 84.*)
Walk through the gardens alongside the museum then up the steps to Café Anton. Continue along Bismarck St.

6 Woermann Haus (Woermann House)

(*See p84.*)
Turn left into Libertina Amathila Ave.

7 Hohenzollernhaus (Hohenzollern House)

Built as a hotel in 1904 (*see p81*), it became so infamous that the magistrates revoked its licence. Facing it across the street, Peter's Antiques is a treasure house of Africana.
Turning left on Hendrik Witbooi St brings you back to Namib-i, and the enticing shops of the Brauhaus Arcade.

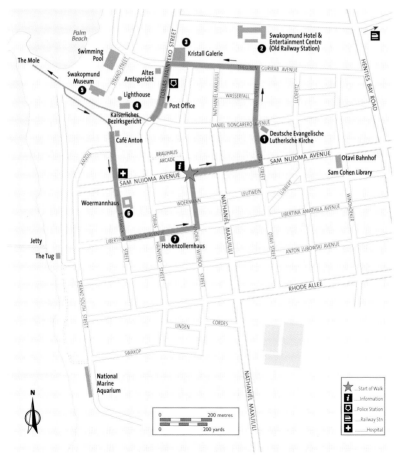

Seals at Cape Cross

Henties Bay

Favoured by the fishing fraternity and as a retirement location, quiet but rapidly expanding Henties Bay increases markedly in population over the Christmas holiday season, as dedicated anglers descend on the coast. It is worth a stop on your way to or from Cape Cross (*see pp84–5*), perhaps for a coffee or meal and the sea views. Golfers will be intrigued by the challenging course there.

The location among dunes by an old riverbed was discovered in 1929 by Major Hentie van der Merwe from Kalkveld, who was searching for water while on a hunting expedition. He loved the place, built himself a shelter from wooden crates and returned every December for a spot of serious fishing. After several years of enjoying the solitude, he began inviting a few friends along, and they referred to it as 'Hentie's Bay'. The name stuck when a settlement grew up there.

Look for the gallows and noose at the entry into the town. The sign beneath it reads: 'Erected in 1978 as an appeal to keep the town and beach clean. Initiated by Frank Atkinson and Willie Cilliers, who respectively settled here in 1969 and 1971 as the first two residents of Henties Bay.' The warning seems to be quite effective.

Two major angling competitions take place here annually, with big prize money on offer. The Penguin Angling Bonanza is on 26 December, and the Fish Festival, held at the end of August, is a two-day event with numerous stalls, games and activities such as car rallying, cycling and fish *braai* (barbecue) competitions to keep the thousands of spectators entertained. *77km (48 miles) northwest from Swakopmund.*

Martin Luther

An old steam tractor, to be seen on the outskirts of town on the road to Windhoek, is a favourite local oddity that's an historical monument. Purchased in Hamburg in 1896 to replace oxen in hauling freight inland, the 280cwt iron 'steam ox' proved to be a bad buy, as it consumed more water than it could carry and constantly got stuck in the sand. The engine broke down in 1897, on the spot where it now stands, and was given the irreverent name *Martin Luther* in reference to the great German reformer's declaration in 1521: 'Here I stand. God help me, I cannot do otherwise.'

Mondesa Township

At the time the black residential area of Mondesa Township was created in the 1950s, as part of the South African regime's apartheid policy of separating the races, it was situated well away from the town centre. Now it is one of Swakopmund's suburbs. An organised tour there will introduce you to some of the residents and includes a drink in a local bar and tastings of traditional foods. Half the cost of the excursion goes directly to the community. *Hata Angu Cultural Tours. Tel: (064) 404 016.*

Saltworks and birdlife

About 7km (4 miles) to the north of Swakopmund, off the C34 salt road to Henties Bay and the Cape Cross Seal Reserve (*see pp84–5*), the pans of the Salt Company attract many species of birds. Residents include avocets, plovers, oystercatchers, grey heron and black-winged stilts. Their numbers are

The *Martin Luther* steam engine

boosted by the numerous migrants arriving between September and April, among them whimbrel, turnstones, sanderling, ringed plover and bar-tailed godwits. Pelicans and cormorants breed on the guano platform off the sandy beach.

Water pumped from the ocean into shallow pans is left to evaporate over a period of 15 months, after which the resulting salt crystals are collected. Oysters are also farmed there. The tracks around the pans are accessible in a saloon car.

Sandwich Harbour

This scenic wilderness, where tall, wind-sculpted dunes meet the beach and the tidal mudflats teem with birdlife, is only accessible in a 4WD vehicle and with an experienced guide. A permit is required to visit and you have to be out of the area before sunset. Several companies offer guided excursions to this isolated and dramatic environment (*see Directory, pp167–8*). *55km (34 miles) south of Walvis Bay.*

Swakop River Mouth

The mix of fresh and salt water at the mouth of the ephemeral Swakop River attracts many birds and allows for a diversity of plant life. A walk along the beach and around the edges of the lagoon takes you among thickets of tamarisk (*Tamarix usneoides*) and

Flamingos are one of the bird species you may encounter in Walvis Bay

extensive reed beds (*Phragmites australis*), dune sand and mudflats. Look out for the bright green mustard tree (*Salvadora persica*), with fleshy leaves that smell strongly of mustard. Its roots are traditionally used for cleaning teeth. Also check out the pencil bush (*Arthraerua leubnitziae*), which channels fog down its grooved stems towards its shallow roots.

Among the many water birds you are likely to encounter are grey heron, moorhen, egret, red-knobbed coot, blacksmith plover, pied avocet, Damara terns and flamingos.

A detailed leaflet, 'Swakop River Mouth Nature Walk', is available from the information office **Namib-i** (*Hendrik Witbooi St, corner Sam Nujoma Ave*).
The Swakop River mouth is on the southern edge of town and the nature trail is about 4km (2¹/₂ miles) long.

Walvis Bay

The road between Swakopmund and Walvis Bay cuts through high desert dunes in shades of ochre and apricot and beaches lapped by the white-crested waves of the blue Atlantic Ocean. About 9km (6 miles) to the north of Walvis Bay, look for the guano platform resting on 1,000 stilts in the sea, where cormorants roost and eastern white pelicans breed.

The only deepwater harbour between Lüderitz and Angola, Walvis Bay ('Bay of Whales') has always been of great strategic importance. Even

RAMSAR CONVENTION

The Ramsar Convention on Wetlands, named after the Iranian city on the Caspian Sea in which this intergovernmental treaty was adopted in 1971, covers all aspects of wetland conservation and its wise and sustainable use. It recognises wetlands as 'ecosystems that are extremely important for biodiversity conservation and for the wellbeing of human communities'. The flagship of the convention is the List of Wetlands of International Importance (the Ramsar List), with wetlands designated for special protection being known as 'Ramsar sites'. The Walvis Bay Wetlands were declared a Ramsar site in June 1995.

after Namibia's independence in 1990, South Africa held on to the enclave and visitors were required to show passports in order to see the myriad birds and marine creatures that abound close to shore. A joint administration agreed in 1992 to abolish border controls and finally in 1994 Walvis Bay joined the rest of independent Namibia. Birdwatching on the lagoon, beach and boat fishing and harbour cruises to spot dolphins and seals are the main attractions here.

Every morning ski-boats leave the Tanker Jetty and Walvis Bay Yacht Club on sightseeing cruises that are among the most popular excursions in the coastal region. They head out to the offshore guano platform known as 'Bird Island' and to see the colony of breeding Cape fur seals at Pelican Point, which is at the end of the long sand spit that shapes the shallow lagoon.

Swakopmund and the coast

Dunes meet the sea between Swakopmund and Walvis Bay, making this area perfect for climbing and sand boarding

Dolphins leap and dive alongside and friendly seals haul themselves aboard the boat with practised ease. Tame enough to touch, they smile around, accept an offering of fish and lap up the admiration before flopping back into the water. Flamingos take to the sky in a patch of pink. When flocks of cormorants come to rest, they appear like a thousand white question marks bobbing in the blue-grey water.

Like Swakopmund, Walvis Bay has its adrenalin adventure activities, including desert quad biking, dune sand boarding and paragliding, windsurfing, parasailing, scenic flights and kayaking on the lagoon. It's a scenic 33km (20 mile) drive south between Swakopmund and the port town of Walvis Bay.
www.walvisbaycc.org.na/tourism.htm

The lagoon

The largest sheet of sheltered shallow water on the Namibian coast, Walvis Bay Lagoon is the most important coastal wetland in Southern Africa. A proclaimed Ramsar site (*see p91*), it ranks in the top three wetlands on the whole continent of Africa. Vast numbers of birds can be seen on the tidal lagoon, along the coast and in the nearby saltpans.

In winter there are as many as 80,000–120,000 birds of between 40 and 50 species. In spring, all the Palaearctic birds from the northern hemisphere arrive, including terns, sanderlings, knots, little stints, grey plovers, bar-tailed godwits and up to 35,000 curlew sandpipers. Over 200,000 birds are counted between September and April, representing 50 to 70 species, while thousands of greater and lesser flamingos can be seen trawling in the shallows all year round.

As well as being a valuable feeding ground for resident breeding birds, intra-African migrants and Arctic-breeding visitors, it is an important nursery site for the threatened African black oystercatcher, which is found only in southern Africa.

There's a fine walk from near the Yacht Club, skirting the lagoon along the esplanade, with excellent birding opportunities.

Dune 7

Just off the airport road on the outskirts of Walvis Bay, Dune 7 is one of the highest dunes in the area. Many people go there to climb it and there's a small picnic site under a few

THE BENGUELA CURRENT

Sweeping from the Antarctic and up the southwestern coast of Africa as far as Angola, the icy Benguela Current affects the climate, flora, fauna and economy of coastal Namibia. As the cooler air above the current meets the hot desert air, a fog or heavy mist is formed. Most mornings it blankets the coastal strip, reaching at least 50km (31 miles) inland, bringing moisture and life to lichens and desert-adapted plants, insects and animals. The nitrogen-rich water supports the plankton on which whales and giant shoals of fish feed, resulting in a hugely important fishing industry for the country.

Ancient *Welwitschia mirabilis* plants grow on the gravel plains

palm trees, which is popular for sundowners.

Welwitschia Trail

A popular half-day drive east of Swakopmund follows a 136km (85 mile) route across the northern gravel plains of the Namib-Naukluft National Park and offers close-up views of the extraordinary *Welwitschia mirabilis* plant (*see pp76–7*). One giant specimen is believed to be over 1,500 years old.

You need a permit to enter the park, which you can get at the **Ministry of Environment and Tourism (MET)** office in Swakopmund. The permit comes with driving directions and explains what you'll see at each of the 13 numbered stone markers. The trail includes viewpoints over the Swakop River Valley's eerie 'Moon Landscape',

where two million years of erosion have revealed 450-million-year-old mica schists and granite. The black streaks snaking across the hills are dolerite that's 120 million years old.

Marker number ten, on the dry riverbed, takes you into a different environment. Here tall trees grow in abundance, fed by the underground water hidden beneath the sand. It is a good spot for a picnic, and tables have been provided in the shade of trees that include camelthorn (*Acacia eriolaba*), ana tree (*Faidherbia albida*) and wild tamarisk (*Tamarix usneoides*).

The desert may initially seem barren but it is full of intriguing life, including ancient lichens that resemble fragments of dead plant material. They are particularly noticeable at markers numbered one and five. Sprinkle a few drops of water on them and watch how they unfold and change colour. Like the welwitschia, they 'feed' on the moisture in the mist that moves in from the sea over the desert at night and blankets the coastal region on most mornings of the year. Lichens grow at a rate of less than 1mm a year and, as the still-visible tracks of an old ox-wagon trail reveal (marker number three), they are very fragile – a reminder of the importance of driving only on existing roads.

The last marker on the trail is an abandoned iron ore mine. It was hand excavated and worked during the 1950s. The Namib-Naukluft National Park carries many relics of prospectors and miners who operated mostly before 1965, but new mine workings are opening up in the area around Swakopmund, which is rich in uranium deposits, and you are likely to see their outlines in the distance as you drive the Welwitschia Trail.

Ministry of Environment and Tourism (MET). Corner Sam Nujoma Ave & Bismarck St. Tel: (064) 404 576. Open: Mon–Fri 8am–1pm & 2–5pm, Sat & Sun 8–11am. There is a charge for the permit.

Wlotzkasbaken

A strange little settlement that, outside of the high summer holiday season, appears to be a ghost town, Wlotzkasbaken is a collection of quirky, brightly painted little holiday homes each sprouting a lofty water tower. They are owned by avid fishermen and are passed down through generations of the same family. Extensive lichen fields can be seen further along the road towards Henties Bay.

31km (19 miles) north of Swakopmund.

Part of the golf course at Henties Bay lies at the mouth of a dry riverbed

Drive: Seals, rhinos and rock art

From the misty, windswept shores of the Skeleton Coast, home to thousands of Cape fur seals, this route turns inland to take you in search of desert-adapted black rhino, among rocks with a 6,000-year legacy of art and to a mountain that seems to burn when the sun sets.

Covering around 900km (560 miles), this is designed as a three-day, round-trip drive from Swakopmund.

Leave Swakopmund on the C34, heading north along this beach-view salt road past the idiosyncratic fishing community at Wlotzkasbaken (see p95). Stop to look at the lichen fields on the right before you reach Henties Bay.

1 Henties Bay

Discover this seaside town beloved by anglers (*see p88*). Follow Duine Rd for a windswept view of the wide sandy riverbed with an immaculate golf course down the centre.
Return to the C34 and continue north.

2 Cape Cross

See the site, marked by stone crosses, where Portuguese navigator Diogo Cão landed in 1486. Beyond it, some 100,000 Cape fur seals inhabit the beach. An amazing, if pungent, sight (*see pp84–5*).
Continue north on the C34.

3 Skeleton Coast Park

Buy your permit for the park at the Ugab River gate (it closes at 3pm). This remote and desolate coastline that once lured ships to their demise holds a strange fascination. Look for the wild tobacco (*Nicotiana glauca*) and the spiky desert food, !nara melon (*Acanthosicyos horridus*), growing in the beds of the Ugab and Huab rivers.
Where the C39 meets the C34 before Torra Bay, turn inland, exiting the park at the Springbokwasser Gate.

The bare landscape of the Skeleton Coast Park

After 93km (58 miles) heading east on the C39, turn left (north) on the C43 for about 40km (25 miles) and follow signs to Palmwag Lodge.

4 Palmwag Concession

The scenery changes dramatically as you pass among crescent-shaped barchan dunes and ancient welwitschia plants into Damaraland's mountains. At the entrance to the huge Palmwag Concession where black rhinos roam, there's a lodge, campsite and the Palmwag Rhino Camp. Next day, join one of the guided game drives or perhaps go rhino tracking.
Drive south on the C43, joining the C39 east towards Khorixas. After about 50km (31 miles) turn right onto the D2612, following the signs for Twyfelfontein.

5 Twyfelfontein

See some of the world's best rock engravings, created 6,000 years ago. Stay overnight at a lodge or campsite nearby (*see p171*) and take in the extraordinary vistas of red rock and blue sky. The Twyfelfontein Country Lodge, built into the mountain rock, even has ancient San rock engravings at the entrance. Book an evening game drive.
Follow the D2612 southeast to join the C35 south towards Uis. Look out for desert elephant along the way. Take the D2359, a right turn about 15km (9 miles) before Uis, towards the Brandberg, a mountain so red that it appears to burn in the setting sun. It's a

28km (17 mile) drive to the Dâureb Mountain Guides office at the foot of the mountain.

6 Brandberg

With Namibia's highest peak (2,573m/8,442ft) and sheltering around 45,000 San (Bushmen) paintings, the Brandberg rises majestically out of the flat plains. It's about an hour's walk from the car park to see the famous White Lady painting, accompanied by a Dâureb guide (*see also pp100–102*). *From Uis continue south on the C35, which joins the C34 coast road by Henties Bay, and return to Swakopmund.*

Distinctly Namibian

Among the 250 mammal species indigenous to Namibia, some stand out as special.

Black-faced impala
(*Aepyceros melampus petersi*)
A graceful antelope with a distinctive dark blaze on its face, the rare black-faced impala is a subspecies that evolved in Kaokoland and across the border in Angola. It is significantly larger and darker than the common impala (*Aepyceros melampus melampus*) and endemic to Namibia.

Black rhinoceros
(*Diceros bicornis bicornis*)
The black, desert-dwelling rhino found in Namibia is an endemic race that lives mainly in barren desert

Black-faced impala

conditions in Kaokoland but is also found in Etosha. Although previously hunted almost to extinction, numbers are increasing thanks to a concerted conservation effort, but it is still an endangered species.

Damara dik-dik
(*Madoqua kirkii damarensis*)
Tiny and doe-eyed, this is the only dik-dik found in southern Africa. A Namibian endemic subspecies of dwarf antelope, they stand only 400mm (16in) tall and weigh about 5kg (11lb).

Desert-adapted elephant
(*Loxodonta africana*)
Genetically identical to the African elephant, although their leaner legs make them look taller, these elephants have adapted their behaviour to survive in the desert. They can go for several days without water (elephants normally drink around 230 litres/405 pints daily) and eat a mere 160kg (353lb) of fodder a day, much less than elephants living in more ideal conditions. Desert elephants dig holes in sandy riverbeds in their hunt for water, are less destructive of their habitat and walk further than any other elephant in Africa in their

Spot the difference: a Mountain zebra lacks the shadow stripes of the more common plains zebra

search for sustenance. The traditional routes and water sources at different times of the year are stored in the head of the matriarch. When she dies the herd is bereft, their library of knowledge gone.

Desert-dwelling giraffe (*Giraffa camelopardalis*)

Giraffe can survive with very little water and like to browse the leaves of acacia trees, which makes them suited to life in the northern Namib Desert, where they range over vast areas. They are particularly partial to the leaves and seedpods of tall ana trees (*Faidherbia albida*) that grow in dry riverbeds.

Mountain zebra (*Equus zebra hartmannae*)

Found only in Namibia and a corner of Angola, the mountain zebra differs from the more common plains or Burchell's zebra (*Equus burchelli*) in several ways. The stripes on its head and body are narrower and more numerous and it doesn't have the 'shadow' stripes of the plains zebra. Other differentiating features include a dewlap (fold of skin hanging from the throat), a white underbelly and a 'gridiron' pattern on its rump. A good climber, it has pointed, extremely hard hooves.

Oryx (*Oryx gazella*)

More widely known by its Afrikaans name 'gemsbok', the African oryx may not be exclusive to Namibia but it is special. So much so that it is depicted on the country's coat of arms. Whether you see a lone gemsbok climbing the dunes at Sossusvlei or a group of them grazing in Etosha, being able to look at their striking features, colours and long, long horns is always a thrill.

Damaraland

Terracotta-coloured mountains, wide plateaux, deep valleys, rocky plains and rolling grassland are all features of Damaraland, a sparsely populated wilderness. Big and remote, it stretches inland for over 200km (124 miles) from the Skeleton Coast National Park in the west to the Etosha National Park in the east and almost 600km (373 miles) from north to south, where it meets the asphalt road to Swakopmund.

These are the ancestral lands of the Damara people, one of the oldest ethnic groups in the country, who speak a complicated language of click sounds that is fascinating to listen to and seemingly impossible to repeat. Here you'll find Namibia's highest mountain and one of the biggest concentrations of ancient rock art in Africa. The site at Twyfelfontein, where over 2,000 engravings, estimated to be 6,000 years old, are incised in the giant rocks, has been awarded World Heritage status by UNESCO.

Damaraland is where rare desert-adapted elephants trek through sand rivers and the last free-roaming black rhino in the world can be seen. Scattered with small settlements and far-flung farms, it is a harsh yet compelling terrain of vast horizons and ruby sunsets that turn rock and mountain such a glowing orange-red that they appear to be on fire.

SOUTHERN DAMARALAND

The highlights here are the great mountains of Spitzkoppe and Brandberg, possible sightings of desert elephants along the dry river course in the Aba-Huab Valley, and the amazing array of rock art engravings at Twyfelfontein. The gravel roads between the sites are accessible to saloon cars. Local transport is donkey cart and if you see people hitch-hiking or looking hopefully for a lift it is because there is no public transport and distances here are very long.

There are only two towns in the area, Uis, a former tin-mining town, and Khorixas. Both are small but are useful for their fuel stations and for stocking up with provisions at the local supermarkets.

Brandberg

An *inselberg* ('island mountain') covering an area of over 750sq km (290sq miles), the Brandberg massif dominates the surrounding plains and glows a fiery red in the setting sun. To local people it is Dâures ('burning mountain').

An active volcano until magma filled its vent around 132 million years ago, it has Namibia's highest peak, Königstein, at 2,573m (8,442ft), and rich galleries of rock paintings, among them the legendary 'White Lady of the Brandberg' (*see p103*). This human figure, painted white from the chest downwards, appears in a large frieze on a rock overhang in the Tsisab ('leopard' in Damara) Ravine.

Some 45,000 individual San (Bushmen) paintings have been discovered in the 1,000 known rock shelters in the massif. The area was designated a national monument in 1951, and there are hopes that it will be accepted for World Heritage status.

The walk to the White Lady site takes 40–60 minutes, depending on the heat and your fitness level, and you must go there with a guide from the Dâureb

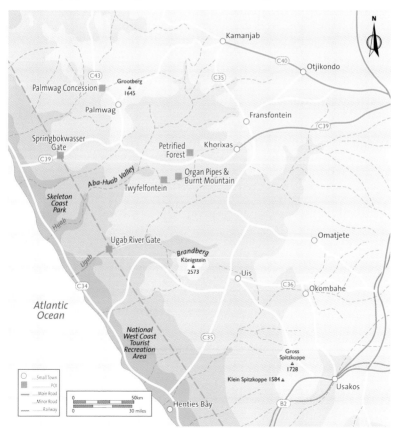

Mountain Guides office at the foot of the mountain. Early morning or late afternoon is the best time for the walk. Wear a hat and carry water with you.
The Brandberg massif is 32km (20 miles) west of Uis. Guides can be contacted through the Uis Tourist Centre (Uis St, Uis. Tel: (064) 504 162. Open: 8am–5pm).

Spitzkoppe

A cluster of mountains rises out of flat desert plains, the highest being Spitzkoppe ('pointed hill') at 600m (1,968ft). Sometimes referred to as 'the Matterhorn of Africa' because of its shape and the difficulty of climbing it, this is the granite core of an ancient volcano, exposed by millions of years of erosion.
Spitzkoppe is 197km (122 miles) northeast of Swakopmund.

Twyfelfontein

At first sight, the red rock hills at Twyfelfontein resemble many others in the vicinity. Rising out of a plain where stands of trees reveal a source of underground water, they were thrown up during the earth's upheavals and carved, shaped and patterned by the elements over aeons: a vista of burnt

The landscape around Twyfelfontein secretes some of the most important rock art in the world

Damaraland

THE WHITE LADY

The discovery of a painting of a 'white lady' in the Brandberg massif in 1917 caused much debate and controversy. Sketched by Reinhardt Maack, the German surveyor who discovered it, a coloured copy appeared in a book published in 1930. Scholars, including Abbé Henri Breuil, an eminent authority on rock art, believed it to have been influenced by Minoan art in Crete, suggesting that the painter had links with Europe, a theory that was widely accepted. Today, the figure, painted white from the chest down, is considered to be of an indigenous person, probably a boy covered in white clay for an initiation ceremony, or a perhaps a shaman.

sienna rock towering against a cobalt blue sky.

What makes them different, however, is that they hide well over 2,000 engravings, incised by early inhabitants. Stone artefacts, tools, fragments of pottery and ostrich eggshell beads aged between 3,450 and 5,850 years have been excavated here.

Twyfelfontein is 70km (44 miles) west of Khorixas.

The San (Bushmen) called this location /Uis-//aes, meaning 'place among packed stones'. The great Etjo sandstone formations provided both shelter and the canvases for pictures depicting animals and beliefs.

Here are dancing kudus and lion men, striding ostriches, laughing baboons, giraffe, rhino, elephant and their spoor as well as geometric images of dotted circles and spheres. This is an outdoor art gallery that has lasted for perhaps 6,000 years and is one of the most important rock-engraving sites on earth.

Rock of ages

The sandstone offers an ideal canvas for engravings. Erosion over millions of years caused large blocks to break away, fracturing along fissures as they tumbled, providing long flat surfaces on which to work. The red colour comes from oxidation in the sand, a process that takes 5,000 years to complete, and forms a thin layer on top of the greyish-white rock beneath. Incising soft rock with a tool of harder rock creates an image that appears white on a red background. Weathering dulls the colours, so originally the contrast would have been much stronger.

The first mention of the hidden rock art by Europeans came in a 1921 land survey report. A farmer, David Levine, moved onto the land in 1946, arriving by donkey cart having followed an elephant track. He named his farm Twyfelfontein ('doubtful spring'), as he was unsure whether the spring could provide enough water for his family and their animals.

The first detailed surveys and excavations were done in the 1960s, which is when the full extent of the engravings and paintings began to be revealed. In 2005, detailed field records documented 2,075 identifiable images, but this is thought to underestimate the true number. In 2007, Twyfelfontein became Namibia's first UNESCO World Heritage Site.

San (Bushmen) rock art

Among the many thousands of San (Bushmen) rock paintings and engravings found in Namibia, the most visited are those at Twyfelfontein (*see pp102–3 & 106–7*), where the 2,000-plus engravings are estimated to be up to 6,000 years old. In 2007, the site gained World Heritage status.

Who these ancient rock artists were is still under discussion, but it is generally believed that the early southern African hunter-gatherer communities used painting and engraving as ways of expressing their beliefs about the supernatural world and recording the experiences of the shamans or medicine people who entered it.

By dancing to rhythmic clapping or chanting, hyperventilation, dehydration or intense concentration, the shaman achieved a state of trance or altered consciousness. Passing through various physical and mental stages, he or she would take on the form of a supernatural creature, often a familiar animal believed to have special powers, such as a rhino, giraffe or elephant, all of which were associated with an abundance of rain. While in the supernatural realm, the shaman had such responsibilities as

making rain, healing the sick and communicating with powerful spirit forces. For people who depended on the land for their survival, and on medicine men for their wellbeing, these were vital tasks.

Sometimes human footprints are paired with hoof prints in the rock art, which may represent a person transforming into the spirit of the animal. Long-legged birds are often shown in a line, straight-backed like people walking in a trance or performing a ritual dance. The Lion Man image at Twyfelfontein has five toes on each paw and his upturned tail ends in a handprint, thus combining the animal and human as the shaman transforms into a lion.

Although many of the engravings appear to depict shamanistic visions, some may have been used for educational purposes, reflecting records of successful hunts, telling of long journeys – why else are seals and penguins portrayed? – or indicating water sources.

The engravings appear in clusters and the sites may have been chosen for specific reasons. Some are in cracks or fissures in the sandstone, perhaps acting as doorways into the supernatural world. The elephant,

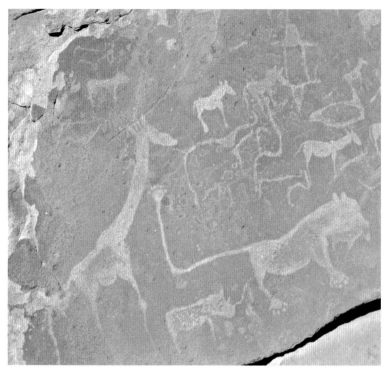

The Lion Man has five toes and a handprint at the end of his tail

rhino, giraffe and various antelope species depicted on the rock would have visited Twyfelfontein during their annual migrations, but the engravings are believed to have been done in the dry season, when a shortage of water would have led people to congregate in the vicinity of the spring and share knowledge and experiences.

It's the fact that there are no people depicted in the oldest engravings that has led to the conviction that the images were inscribed for ritual purposes. The more recent (2,000-year-old) San paintings in caves on the site show people engaged in activities including dancing and hunting.

Of the meaning of the geometric symbols, the lines, holes and circles, little is known or understood. Some say the mix of lines and dots is an early form of calendar, and that the circles with central hole-like dots represent water-source locations. At one place there are circles within circles that have been shown to be a good representation of the solar system as it would have been seen approximately 4,000 years ago.

The basaltic Organ Pipes can be 5m (16ft) high

Visitors Centre

In natural earth colours of red and rust, the Visitors Centre blends in with the landscape. Built without cement and using mainly natural and recycled materials, it reflects the spirit of the hunter-gatherers who left no impact on the environment when they moved on.

The walls are formed from hand-packed wire gabion baskets filled with local sandstone rubble. The roof is covered with 'tiles' cut from recycled oil drums and insulated with a ceiling of reed mats cut and woven as part of an employment project. Inside, well-presented displays give information on the flora and fauna of the surroundings, the history of the site and the meaning of the ancient engravings.

To visit the rock engravings you must call first at the Visitors Centre, where a trained local guide will accompany you to the sites. There are two routes to choose from, both entailing some stiff clambering among the rocks. The longer route takes in rock paintings as well as engravings. The best times to visit are early morning and late afternoon. Try to avoid the heat and harsh light of midday. There's no shade at the site so wear a hat, good walking shoes and carry water.

For descriptions of three sites worth visiting in the area near Twyfelfontein – the Petrified Forest, Organ Pipes and Burnt Mountain – see the driving route (*pp108–9*).

Open: 8am–5pm. www.nhc-nam.org

NORTHERN DAMARALAND

Huge, flat-topped mountains and wide valleys form a spectacular landscape to the north of the Huab River. Herds of springbok, oryx and Hartmann's mountain zebra roam this vast, seemingly almost deserted region, which receives little rainfall. Spiky *Euphorbia damarana* bushes punctuate the sparse grasslands. Endemic to the region, they contain a milky-white latex that is highly poisonous to all except kudu and black rhino.

Here, through the formation of conservancies and concession areas, tourism and local communities work hand in hand to preserve wildlife and improve living conditions for the people who try to eke out a living through subsistence farming. There are some very successful community-run campsites and joint ventures with private lodges. Community game guards are employed to ensure no illegal hunting takes place, and local farmers are compensated when wildlife destroys their precarious livelihoods.

Ecotourism brings much-needed income and jobs. Communities receive a percentage of the revenue from the lodges as well as the benefits of employment and training. The guides at the lodges are excellent and at least a two-night stay is needed to fully appreciate their knowledge of the plants, birds and animals as they take you on game drives and rhino-tracking expeditions in remote locations.

The vast Palmwag Concession, which has a lodge and camp (*see Directory, p171*), is home to the desert-adapted black rhino. Known to cover some 2,500sq km (965sq miles) in search of food, they can climb high onto mountain ledges out of the heat of the valley and go without water for four days. They are protected by the Save the Rhino Trust, and rhino-tracking expeditions are possible from the Palmwag Rhino Camp.

Perched dramatically on the rim of the Entendeka Plateau at the very top of the Grootberg Pass, with stunning views down a wide, sweeping gold and red rock valley, Grootberg Lodge (*see Directory, pp170–71*) is in the Khoadi//Hôas Conservancy. It is owned by the conservancy (the name means 'elephants' corner') and the plan is for local people to be running the lodge in future. It's a magical place, and from here you can do guided walks along the plateau, go horse riding, elephant and rhino tracking, and also visit villages.

Drive: Twyfelfontein rock art and intriguing sights

The rock engravings at Twyfelfontein are world famous and are on most people's 'must-see' list when planning an itinerary. Taking you through an extraordinary desert landscape where orange-red rocks rise into a cobalt-blue sky, this drive shows you some amazing sights.

This is a day excursion covering about 100km (62 miles).

From Khorixas, drive west along the C39 road for about 45km (28 miles), when you will see the Petrified Forest on your right.

1 Petrified Forest

Some 50 fossilised tree trunks, ancient ancestors of conifers and dated to around 280 million years old, lie scattered on a sandstone rise. They were deposited there by meltwaters towards the end of a long period of Ice Age and got buried under a thick layer of sand and rubble. The 'living fossil' *Welwitschia mirabilis* plant grows here, too, which adds to the prehistoric feel of the place. *Admission charge includes guide. Continue west on the C39. Turn left onto the D2612 (Twyfelfontein) for about 15km (9 miles) and follow the turn-off onto the D3214. Drive through the dry Aba-Huab riverbed. After the Aba-Huab Community Campsite sign, continue for a further 5km (3 miles) to where a junction is clearly marked to the Twyfelfontein rock engravings.*

2 Twyfelfontein

The Visitors Centre (*see p106*) has lots of information on the engravings, the site's history and the local flora and fauna, also a refreshment kiosk and a seating area with tables. A local guide will accompany you on the pathways among the rocks that lead up to the engravings. The 'Dancing Kudu' route includes a visit to San rock paintings as well as engravings and takes about an hour. The 'Lion Man' route takes about 45 minutes. Be sure to wear a hat and carry water.

Drive back the way you came. After 5km (3 miles) the road forks onto the D3254, signed for Burnt Mountain. After about 3km (2 miles) there's a small gorge to your left. Look for a slate with the handwritten word 'Orellpype' ('organ pipes' in Afrikaans).

3 Organ Pipes

Rows of perpendicular dolerite columns, known as the Organ Pipes, line the shallow gorge. They were formed about 125 million years ago from cooling and contracting magma that penetrated vertically into the parallel rock layers on top of it and solidified into polygonal rock columns. The best way to see this strange natural phenomenon is to walk along the sandy riverbed, where the tightly packed angular columns, some up to 5m (16ft) tall, rise up on both sides.

Continue along the D3254 and you'll soon see the Burnt Mountain.

4 Burnt Mountain

To the casual observer, the mountain resembles a slag heap, but for anyone interested in geology it is fascinating. Its story goes back around 125 million years when vast volumes of basaltic magna at temperatures above 1,000°C (1,832°F) pushed up towards the earth's surface and through the existing shale, igniting the organic material which then vaporised, and burning the shale into a black 'crust' of compacted rock. The purple-red shiny patches are the result of erosion exposing iron and manganese, the yellow colour is sulphur and the blue iron-copper oxides.

Return to the D2612.

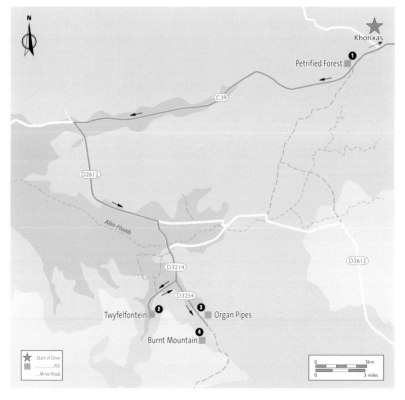

Himba children love wearing, and making, jewellery

SAVE THE RHINO TRUST

In the 1980s, when South African Defence Force personnel and poachers were hunting elephant and desert-adapted black rhino almost to extinction in the arid northwest, Rudi Loutit and his late wife Blythe started a pressure group in an attempt to stop the slaughter. Eventually they succeeded and, ever since, Save the Rhino Trust has pioneered conservation in the region, employing community game guards and ranger-trackers and operating daily patrols by vehicle and camel, monitoring and protecting the rhino. Rhino numbers have doubled and the trust's research and database are considered to be the most comprehensive source on rhino population in the world.

Kaokoland

In the extreme northwest of Namibia, remote, inhospitable Kaokoland spans 40,000sq km (15,444sq miles) and stretches up to the border with Angola. Rugged, arid and mountainous, with few facilities and no good roads, it is not a region to consider lightly. Convoys of well-equipped 4WD vehicles can travel there, but it is best explored with a specialist Kaokoland tour operator, such as **Namibia Travel Connection** (*Tel: (061) 246 247*).

For more information about the region, visit *www.namibiatourism.com.na*

Damaraland

Himba

Kaokoland is home to the Himba, a semi-nomadic pastoral people who live in small settlements and wander with their cattle and goats in search of water and grazing. Much photographed for their beauty and traditional way of living and dressing, they continue with long-held customs while the world around them changes. Cattle, symbols of status and wealth, are central to their lives.

A Himba village is made up of a collection of beehive-shaped huts, built from the branches of mopane trees, then covered with a mixture of mud and dung, and a protected *kraal* (enclosure) for the animals. A ritual fire, the *okoruwo*, burns constantly in front of the headman's hut and is a sacred place that provides contact with the ancestors.

Himba women cover their skin in a thick layer of red ochre that gives them protection against the sun and keeps them looking remarkably smooth-skinned. Their hair, woven, braided and plaited into elaborate styles, also receives the ochre treatment. Married women can be distinguished by the soft headpiece made of animal skin and a neck ornament of leather with a conch shell at the front and metal-studded panels that hang down at the back. Himba women wear a lot of heavy and distinctive jewellery that looks very dramatic against their glowing, russet-coloured skin. Even the youngest children are adorned with simple jewellery such as necklaces woven from palm leaves.

DESERT ELEPHANTS

It's an exciting moment when you come across the desert elephants that roam the northwest of Namibia. One of only two known populations of desert-dwelling elephants in the world (the other is in Mali, West Africa), their leaner legs and bigger feet make them look taller than their cousins on the plains. They move fast and may wander up to 60km (37 miles) a day in search of ground water, digging holes known as 'gorras' in the sand to access it, and the 160kg (353lb) of fodder they consume daily.

Their routes take them through bush, along the wide sandy beds of ephemeral rivers and across farms where they cause havoc in the local population. Look for the stones piled up around boreholes and water tanks, placed there by farmers to deter elephants from demolishing their water sources.

Many of the lodges and camps in the Twyfelfontein area offer excursions into the desert to search for the elephants. If you are driving a saloon car this is a good option. You may be fortunate to see them from the road while crossing the Aba Huab Valley, but will need a 4WD vehicle to follow their tracks across the sand.

If you are not travelling into Kaokoland, there are Himba villages that can be seen from northern Damaraland and several lodges arrange guided visits. One settlement is on the farm Gelbingen, owned by Volker and Andrea Hoth, near the small town of Kamanjab. Andrea will tell you how the Himba people came to live on their farm and accompany you into the settlement where the women sell their handmade jewellery and crafts.

Gelbingen Guest Farm.
Tel: (067) 330 277.

Namibia's Big Eight: stars of the bush

The term 'Big Five' was coined by trophy hunters who considered elephant, lion, leopard, rhinoceros and buffalo the most dangerous animals to kill. Safari-goers who shoot with cameras would put the photogenic cheetah, zebra and giraffe pretty high on their wishlist. In Namibia you have a good chance of seeing them all – and a whole lot more.

African elephant (*Loxodonta africana*)

You have only to watch an elephant demolish or uproot a tree to realise that after man, elephants are the most destructive of their environment. They eat up to 300kg (661lb) of leaves, roots, bark, grasses and fruit each day, causing havoc in the process. Elephants are a matriarchal society, with the oldest female leading a herd of nine to eleven closely related females and their calves.

African lion (*Panthera leo*)

The largest African carnivore and the only cat to live in organised social groups, lions live in prides of at least four to six adults and their young. They hunt mainly at night and spend much of the day resting and sleeping in the shade. The female lacks the distinctive mane of the male lion who, when fully grown, can weigh 240kg (529lb), have a body length of 2.5m (8ft) and stand 1.2m (4ft) at the shoulder.

Black rhinoceros (*Diceros bicornis bicornis*)

Endemic to Namibia (see p98), the desert-adapted black rhino is under threat, although it is the focus of conservation efforts. Its pointed prehensile upper lip distinguishes it from the more numerous square-lipped white rhinoceros (*Ceratotherium simum*), which also lives in Namibia. Both species are in fact grey in colour.

Blue wildebeest (*Connochaetes taurinus*)

Also known as 'brindled gnu' for the dark vertical stripes on their necks and flanks, they appear strange characters with their humped shoulders, sloping backs and rocking-horse gait. Gregarious creatures, blue wildebeest live in herds of 30 or more and have the habit of snorting and tossing their massive heads.

Blue wildebeest are also known as 'brindled gnu'

Cheetah (*Acinonyx jubatus*)

With its long, muscular and streamlined body, the cheetah was built for speed and can sprint up to 113kph (70mph) over short distances. Shy and secretive, cheetahs live a mainly solitary existence and, unlike most cats, choose to hunt during the day, preferring early morning or late afternoon to seek their favourite food of small antelopes. Cheetah cubs are very vulnerable and have to be taught to hunt. The cheetah may not roar like a lion, but it purrs very loudly.

Giraffe (*Giraffa camelopardis*)

The world's tallest (up to 5.5m/18ft) land animal uses its rubbery lips and very long tongue to harvest the highest leaves from prickly acacia trees. The giraffe may have an ungainly gait but it can reach speeds of 56kph (35mph).

Leopard (*Panthera pardus*)

Solitary and secretive, the elusive leopard can be difficult to spot, as its tawny, rosette-patterned coat provides excellent camouflage in the long grass or thick bush in the rocky surroundings that they favour as a habitat. A cunning and stealthy hunter, the leopard will often drag kills bigger than itself up into the branches of a tree, where it can return to eat in relative safety.

Zebra (*Equus burchelli*)

The zebra's stripes of black, white and shadow brown are as individual as a human's fingerprint. Highly sociable animals, they live in harems of females led by a stallion and can be seen in large groups across grass and woodland savannah, often accompanied by wildebeest.

Etosha National Park

Covering an area of 22,912sq km (8,846sq miles), Etosha is one of the world's great game reserves. At its heart lies the vast Etosha Pan, a shallow inland lake that dried up millions of years ago. Stretching for 110km (68 miles) east to west and 60km (37 miles) north to south, it covers some 4,730sq km (1,830sq miles) of glistening and shimmering, flat silvery-white sand and salt where dust devils dance and mirages deceive the eye. The pan gave the park its name: 'Etosha' means 'great white place'.

The landscape along the southern reaches of the pan, where the roads are, varies from mopane woodland to wide-open plains with hardly a tree in sight. Giraffe, kudu and eland browse in the woodlands; springbok, oryx, zebra and blue wildebeest graze the plains. Lion stalk through long grass, elephant demolish trees, ostrich pad across the pan and tiny, doe-eyed Damara dik-dik peek out from prickly bush. Rhino, black and white, keep their distance; leopards have secret hideaways.

Etosha supports 114 mammal species and 340 species of birds. Blue cranes breed there, kori bustards stride purposefully, lappet-faced and African white-backed vultures nest atop trees, and martial, Bateleur and tawny eagles soar gracefully high in the sky. Greater and lesser flamingos descend on the pan in seasons of good rain. You can almost set your watch by the flocks of double-banded sandgrouse that swoop noisily into rest-camp waterholes after sunset.

Waterholes are good places to see large numbers of animals in one place. It's a great thrill to see elephants taking a dust and mud bath or giraffe descending on bended knee to slake their thirst.

The passing parade does not stop at sunset. To sit quietly by a floodlit waterhole, wrapped in the darkness of night, is to feel a sense of theatre as elephants enter stage right, zebra canter off, stage left, and a black rhino appears as an unannounced star attraction.

TOP TEN WATERHOLES

1 Okaukuejo (rest camp)
2 Olifantsbad
3 Rietfontein
4 Halali (rest camp)
5 Goas
6 Kalkheuwel
7 Chudop
8 Klein Namutoni
9 Namutoni (rest camp)
10 Tsumcor

Etosha National Park

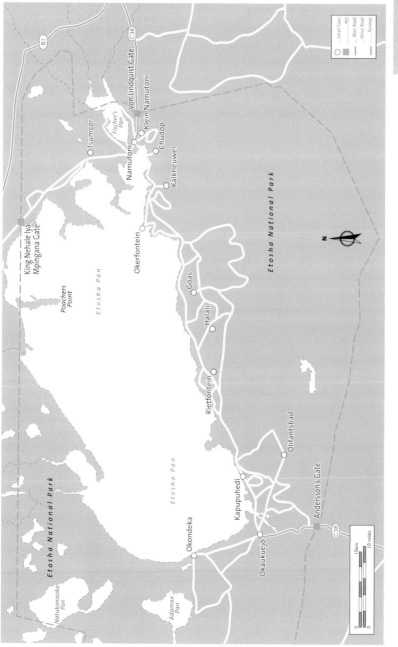

STAYING INSIDE THE PARK

There are three rest camps (resorts) within the park, and while they all have very smart room and bungalow accommodation, campsites and similar facilities (restaurant, bar, swimming pool, filling station and shops), each has its own distinctive atmosphere and character.

The biggest and busiest is **Okaukuejo** (originally Okakwiya, 'the woman who has a child every year'), 11km (7 miles) from the Andersson's Gate (*see Directory, p172*). The park's administrative centre and home to the research and conservation management Ecological Institute, its facilities include a post office and internet centre and you can climb the tall water tower for panoramic views. **Namutoni** (originally Omutjamatinda in Herero, 'the strong water coming from a raised place'), 10km (6 miles) from the Von Lindquist Gate in the east and set around a splendid old fort, is the most stylish and atmospheric (*see Directory, p172*).

ESSENTIAL THINGS TO KNOW ABOUT ETOSHA

- The park opens at sunrise and closes at sunset. Exact times are clearly shown at both gates. You get your entry permit at the gate and pay for it at the first rest camp you come to. The rest camp reception offices follow the same hours, so if you are staying overnight in the park be sure to arrive well before sunset to allow 30 minutes' travelling time between the entry gate and the resorts. The check-in process can take a while.

- The roads are gravel and the speed limit is 60kph (37mph). You must stay in your car at all times (except at the designated toilet stops) and never drive off-road. Animals have the right of way.

- Early morning and after 3pm are the best times for game-viewing drives. Aim to be back at your rest camp by around midday and relax in the shade by the camp's waterhole.

- You are more likely to see the largest concentrations of game in the dry season, roughly June to mid-November, especially gathered around the waterholes. During and after the rains (a great time for bird-watching), the animals tend to disperse into the dense green bush and are less easy to spot. Also, many migrate into areas of the park that are not open to the public.

Namutoni Fort

Waterholes provide some of the best game spotting in Etosha

Midway (around 70km/43 miles) between them, **Halali** ('the hunt is over') is set among mopane trees (*see Directory, pp171–2*).

Each rest camp has a waterhole that is floodlit at night, which makes staying in park accommodation particularly appealing. The big waterhole at Okaukuejo, which attracts large numbers of animals, is often visited at night by black rhino and is one of the best places to see this rare and secretive beast.

Etosha never feels crowded, even in high season. Often you can travel for hours and hardly see another vehicle.

The park was designed for visitors to drive themselves around – the gravel roads can all be driven in a saloon car – and it really is the best way to experience the landscape and the animals. With your own transport you are free to spend as long as you like at a waterhole or watching, for example, a pride of lions snoozing in the shade with their young playing around them. But if time is short or you are on an organised tour, buses can also provide plentiful game viewing (small group tours are best) and the upmarket lodges (*see Directory, p172*) on the outskirts of the park all offer day excursions in their own vehicles.

Namibia's north: the Caprivi Strip

Bounded by four big rivers, the Caprivi Strip is a narrow band of land, 450km (280 miles) long and 100km (62 miles) at its widest, separating the countries of Angola and Zambia in the north and Botswana in the south. Lush and green, it seems like another country. It has perennial rivers and forests and offers different vegetation, animal and birdlife from the arid lands to the south. This is the only part of Namibia with plentiful water, which supports a large population farming fertile pastures and much wildlife.

With traditional villages, circular huts, cattle *kraal* (protected enclosures) and roadside fruit and vegetable sellers, Caprivi is more like most people's image of Africa. There are many similarities with its neighbours. Even the main language spoken by Caprivians – Lozi – is the language of the Lozi people in Zambia.

Once part of the British Protectorate of Bechuanaland (Botswana), it was ceded to Germany during the 'Scramble for Africa' (*see p8*) and named after the then German chancellor, Count Georg Leo von Caprivi. For a brief spell after World War I, the region again became part of Bechuanaland, but in 1929 was returned to South West Africa, by then under South African administration. On the map it appears like an appendage or artificial limb attached to the main body of Namibia.

The landscape is a mosaic of riverine forests and woodlands, swamps and rivers, channels and floodplains. Except for the main asphalt road – often referred to as the 'Golden Highway' – this is mostly 4WD country.

With virtually no tourist infrastructure, the Caprivi Strip's game reserves are little visited and can be difficult terrain to access even by experienced 4WD drivers. The national parks of Mudumu and Mamili are wildernesses crisscrossed by

The rare wild dog can be spotted in the Caprivi Strip

Sunset over the Caprivi Strip

waterways. Both host an extraordinary variety of birds, with 400 species found in Mudumu, which is also visited by elephant, buffalo, such seldom-seen antelope as roan, sable, red lechwe and sitatunga, and also rare African wild dog. Naturally, crocodiles and hippos are permanent residents.

Mahango National Park is more accessible. On the banks of the Okavango River, it is a world of papyrus reed beds, wild date palm forests, lush riverine vegetation and pristine Kalahari sand, which makes for a prolific and diverse collection of birds, with probably the best sightings in Namibia. There is no accommodation in the park, but several upmarket lodges and a campsite are nearby.

Impalila Island in the easternmost corner of Namibia is known as 'the one island in Africa where four countries meet'. About 11km (7 miles) long and 4km (2½ miles) wide, it can be reached by boat from Kasane in Botswana. Wildlife, villages, good walking trails, fishing, exploring inlets in a *moroko* (dugout canoe) and upmarket lodges are features of this remote location at the meeting point of the Zambezi and Chobe rivers.

From the busy town of Katima Mulilo, the regional administrative centre on the banks of the Zambezi River, a road bridge links Namibia with Zambia. Then it's just a three-hour drive to the Victoria Falls.

Visit *www.namibia-travel.net* for more details.

Getting away from it all

Namibia is nature on a grand scale, with far horizons and vistas that not even a wide-angle camera lens can capture. A sense of space and freedom is one of the great joys of being in this quite spectacular corner of Africa. Here you travel on almost empty roads and relish the clear, unpolluted air. By day the sky is so blue the colour seems unreal; by night it is spread with dazzling galaxies of stars.

Some areas are so remote that they can only be accessed by fly-in safaris or in a convoy of at least two fully equipped 4WD vehicles, with GPS and a good local guide. Two stand out as remarkable experiences.

BUSHMANLAND

An almost blank area bordering on Botswana appears on the map in Namibia's northeast. Bushmanland (a name that dates back to South African rule but still in general use) covers a wilderness area of around 18,000sq km (6,950sq miles) of vegetated Kalahari sand and is home to scattered communities of Ju/'hoansi (San or !Kung Bushmen). Ju/'hoansi, pronounced 'Zhu-wahnsi', means 'real people'.

The administrative centre is at Tsumkwe, a collection of buildings on the C44 about 300km (186 miles) east of Grootfontein. With no fuel station and few provisions available, it's important that your 4WD is very well

supplied and stocked for your whole trip before leaving Grootfontein.

Tsumkwe is at the centre of the 9,003sq km (3,476sq mile) Nyae Nyae Conservancy where the Ju/'hoan people have the right to utilise the wildlife in the area by receiving an income from a hunting concession. The Conservancy office in Tsumkwe can offer advice on travelling in the area and arrange a guide from the community. Authentic Bushmen crafts are sold in the shop next door.

Staying at Nhoma Camp (*see p173*), close to the village of //Nhoq'ma 80km (50 miles) from Tsumkwe, is the ideal way to experience Bushman life and learn about their extraordinary hunting and survival skills. There are just six twin safari tents, each with an adjoining grass-enclosed shower room, set among Zambesi teak trees. Hunters involve guests as they teach and demonstrate such traditional skills as fire making, setting traps and gathering wild food. In the evening the whole village participates in traditional games, followed by healing dances.

It's a simple camp with no luxuries, but it offers an unforgettable experience of a hunter-gatherer culture so very different from our own.

The Khaudum National Park, Namibia's wildest, most remote game reserve, lies in the north of Bushmanland. It is tough driving country, strictly for those experienced in 4WD off-road driving on soft sand. With only the most basic of camping sites, you need to come well prepared with sufficient food, water and fuel to last several days. Entry is restricted to a minimum of two well-equipped 4WD vehicles travelling together, and the tracks through the reserve are not passable after rain.

Game to be spotted here includes tsessebe, red hartebeest, blue wildebeest and rare wild dog, as well as elephant, giraffe and roan antelope. There are no fences in the Park, which receives so few visitors that the animals are not accustomed to the presence of humans or the sound of vehicles. The magic is in the wilderness environment.

SAFARIS IN THE SKELETON COAST NATIONAL PARK

Wild and desolate, the northern section of the Skeleton Coast National Park stretching up into Angola has a stark beauty that attracts those in search of a remote wilderness experience.

In this narrow tract of coastline, about 32km (20 miles) wide, are high dunes that roar, rumble and reverberate when disturbed and a deep canyon where soft sand has been sculpted by the elements into shapes resembling castles and ancient temples.

Getting away from it all

Euphorbia damarana

For centuries this treacherous coast of reefs, swirling sea fogs and shifting sands has lured ships to their doom. Pounded by the relentless sea and sandblasted by wind, remnants of their wrecks lie above the tide line, bleached and shaped into contorted sculptures.

Despite the harsh environment the Skeleton Coast sustains life, from great colonies of Cape fur seals on beaches where black-backed jackal and brown hyena roam, to the strange welwitschia plant, lithops (flowering succulents that resemble stones) and over 100 species of lichen on the gravel plains.

Desert oases, created by freshwater springs, support springbok, oryx, giraffe, ostrich and the rare desert-adapted elephant. Several of Namibia's desert endemic birds are found here, including the tractrac chat, Rüppell's khoraan and Gray's lark. Over 200 bird species have been recorded in the area.

CROSSING BORDERS

South Africa's Northern Cape region sweeps up against Namibia's southern and eastern borders. In the far north, the Kavango River fans out to form Botswana's world-famous wetlands, the Okavango Delta. Meanwhile, the Zambezi River rushes onwards to power over the Victoria Falls in neighbouring Zambia and Zimbabwe. Roads that head straight for numerous border posts make Namibia's neighbours easy to reach.

It is such a fragile ecosystem that access to this part of the National Park is restricted to small-group fly-in safaris. There are two options and both operators employ expert guides who are passionate about this strange and mysterious, little-visited region.

Skeleton Coast Safaris (*see p173*) has three fully equipped tented camps – the tents have en-suite bucket showers and flush toilets – and you spend one night in each of them on four-day safaris

Sunrise over the Klip River Valley, the view from Grootberg Lodge

Springbok take advantage of shade afforded by the occasional tree

from Windhoek. Group sizes are a minimum of two and a maximum of eight people.

In between the scenic flights, up the coast and inland, there are 4WD excursions to explore the diverse flora and fauna found among the red lava and yellow sandstone around the Huab River, to roaring dunes and to beaches where bleached whale bones are scattered across pebbles of agate, lava, granite and quartz. A visit is made to a settlement of the nomadic Himba people who still live and dress in the traditional ways, and there's a boat trip on the Kunene River, Namibia's border with Angola, observing birdlife and probably crocodiles, too.

With Wilderness Safaris (*see p173*) you are based at the company's Skeleton Coast Camp, set in their 16,400sq km (6,332sq mile) private concession within the Skeleton Coast National Park. The camp, built on an island in the dry Khumib riverbed, has six quite luxurious tents with spacious bedrooms and en-suite bathrooms.

From there you set out each day in 4WD vehicles on nature drives and walks, excursions to a seal colony and natural springs, visits to a remote Himba village in neighbouring Kaokoland, to the roaring dunes and lichen fields, also tracking desert elephants if they are in the area at the time.

For fly-in safaris, your luggage must be packed in a soft-sided carry bag and weigh not more than 10kg (22lbs).

The Okavango Delta in Botswana

Botswana

You can drive into Botswana from the Caprivi Strip (*see pp118–19*), but the most convenient way to reach the superb riverside lodges and luxurious tented camps in the Okavango Delta is to fly from Windhoek to Maun. From there you'll be collected by light aircraft for a short flight to the lodge's private landing strip.

By flying you get an eagle-eye view of the delta, which is pretty special. It is one of the world's biggest inland waterways and spans over 16,000sq km (6,180sq miles). If the budget doesn't stretch to luxury, there's a good choice of assisted camping safaris.

In this mosaic of land and water, of water-lily lagoons and palm-tree islands, days can be spent quietly gliding through papyrus-fringed channels in a *mokoro* (dugout canoe), on game drives, guided walks or fishing for bream and tiger fish. Fish eagles cry overhead, and African jacanas hop lightly between lily pads.

The wildlife is abundant here, with sightings of aquatic antelope such as red lechwe and the rare and shy sitatunga. Hippos create channels among the reeds, crocodiles bask on sunny banks, elephant emerge from the bush and giraffes lope inelegantly into view. There are buffalo here, too, lion sometimes, and the birdlife is amazing. From giant saddle-billed and marabou storks, pelicans and Goliath herons to smaller brethren such as pied and malachite kingfishers, greenshanks and plovers, the delta seems a never-ending festival of life on the wing.

Botswana Tourism.

www.botswana-tourism.gov.bw

South Africa

Accessed through the 24-hour Ariamsvlei border post on the Karasburg-Upington road in the southwest corner of South Africa, Upington is the gateway to the 'Cape Namibia Route' that leads all the way south to Cape Town.

The town of Upington overlooks lush island vineyards in the broad Orange River, which forms Namibia's border with South Africa. Here vivid green vineyards are set against a red sand and desert landscape. There's nothing quite like relaxing with a glass or two of local red wine as you watch the setting sun scatter the river's blue waters with flamboyant shades of red and purple.

The Orange River meanders on until, channelled into an 18km long (11 mile) ravine, it plunges, thunderously and tumultuously, into a giant rift in the earth's surface at Augrabies Falls. Crashing over high ledges, this is among the world's largest waterfalls. It heads on towards the South Atlantic Ocean through the remote and rugged mountains of the Richtersveld National Park and its

sandy plains, where strange-looking plants reach for the life-giving fogs that roll in from the sea.

If you drive all the way south on the main B1 road from Windhoek and cross the border at Noordoewer, you'll come to the old copper-mining town of Springbok in the heart of Namaqualand. The time to do this is in early spring, when the normally arid landscape is transformed by millions of cheerful daisies and vibrant mesembryanthemums. After the winter rains (usually mid-Aug–mid-Sept) so many wild flowers coat the area that the mountains appear to be floating in a sea of colour.

Cape Namibia Route.

www.capenamibia.com

South African Tourist Board.

www.southafrica.net

On the South African side of the Orange River, the Augrabies Falls are a spectacular sight

When to go

With more than 300 days of sunshine, Namibia is a year-round destination. There's really no bad time to visit the country. The two main seasons are winter (May–Sept) and summer (Dec–Mar), with the intermediate months distinctly spring-like or autumnal. Rainfall is erratic, but is most likely to fall between December and March.

Climate conditions do vary between regions, but most of Namibia is arid or semi-arid desert and receives little rainfall. The coast and the Caprivi Strip present the most marked differences.

The cold Benguela Current affects the weather at the coast. When the hot air from the interior meets the cold air off the ocean, a morning fog forms and bathes the coast for up to 60km (37 miles) inland with a mist that supports the Namib Desert's endemic flora and fauna. This region receives little rain, on average a mere 15mm (²⁄₃in) a year. Temperatures at the coast are comfortable all year round. In contrast, rainfall in the Caprivi Strip averages 700mm (28in) and humidity can be quite high during the rainy season.

WEATHER CONVERSION CHART

25.4mm = 1 inch
°F = 1.8 × °C + 32

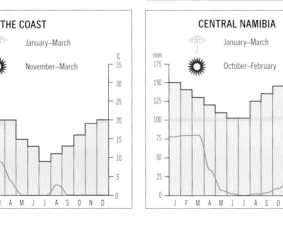

The hottest months are December, January and February, when temperatures in the arid interior can top 40°C (104°F). Being a desert environment, the country experiences big variations in temperature between day and night, from winter to summer, and depending on the height above sea level.

In the 'dry season' between April and September, days are warm, skies are clear and temperatures average around 25°C (77°F). They drop considerably at night, especially in July when frost is common in the desert and at higher elevations. Temperatures start rising in October and November, with little likelihood of rain.

Leading up to the 'wet season', scanning the skies for tell-tale clouds, everyone longs for the arrival of the rains to cool the air and revitalise the vegetation. There may be some rainfall in December and by March most areas of Namibia will have received their allocation for the year. Mostly it falls in heavy downfalls or thunderstorms of quite short duration, but occasionally there are periods when dry riverbeds become raging torrents, making gravel roads impassable in a saloon car. On a typical rainy day, however, you are likely to wake up to blue skies. Clouds start appearing in the afternoon, there's a torrential downpour for an hour or so, then by the early evening the sky is clear again.

Best times to visit

The best time to see plentiful game in the Etosha National Park is between July and November, when the vegetation is dry and animals move closer to waterholes sited in rest camps and near to the roads. During and after the rains, game can be much harder to find, either because the animals are hidden by the lush vegetation or because they have migrated to areas of the park that are not accessible to visitors. For avid birdwatchers, however, the rainy season offers a cornucopia of summer migrants.

The cooler days in May to September are best for hiking.

Accommodation in Namibia gets heavily booked during the Namibian school holidays (late Apr–late May, mid-Aug–early Sept, and early Dec–mid-Jan) and the coast is very busy in December and January. Although they are the coldest periods of the year (particularly at night), July, August and early September are popular months with European (especially German) visitors, as they coincide with the long school holidays. October, too, can see upmarket lodges at their busiest.

When to go

Dry riverbeds can become raging torrents

Getting around

Namibia is a vast country and distances between towns and scenic highlights are long. Most visitors join organised tours or plan self-drive itineraries. A well-established network of over 42,000km (26,000 miles) of road, of which 5,500km (3,420 miles) is asphalt, crisscrosses the country. The majority of the 37,000km (22,990 miles) of gravel and dirt roads are well maintained. Traffic is light and signposting is good. Alternatively, small planes make short work of the long distances.

By air

Flying is the quickest, if not the cheapest, way to connect with main centres. **Air Namibia** links Windhoek's Eros Airport with Lüderitz, Walvis Bay, Ondangwo in the far north and Katima Mulilo in the Caprivi Strip, also Lüderitz with Walvis Bay.

A number of local charter services operate flights and tours by light aircraft. The airport at Swakopmund is always busy with charters. Many of the upmarket lodges have their own landing strips and it is now possible to do fly-in safaris between lodges. **Namibia Travel Connection** can tailor-make such a trip or combine light aircraft flights with self-drive itineraries. This combination is a good time-saving option that still gives you the freedom to explore on your own.

Charter flights are useful for short breaks. The **Dune Hopper** departs daily from Windhoek and Swakopmund with two- to five-night

stays in privately owned lodges and camps in the NamibRand Nature Reserve and Sossusvlei.
Air Namibia. Tel: (061) 299 6333.
www.airnamibia.com.na
Namibia Travel Connection.
Tel: (061) 246 427.
www.namibiatravel.com
Dune Hopper. Tel: (061) 234 793.
www.dunehopper.com

Namibia straddles the Tropic of Capricorn

International flights arrive at Windhoek's modern Hosea Kutako airport

By car

Namibia's asphalt roads are wide and in good condition, most of the gravel roads are well maintained and traffic is light. Driving is on the left. You need to be 23 or over to hire a car and have a photocard driving licence or International Driving Permit. The speed limit on asphalt roads is 120kph (75mph), on gravel roads 80kph (50mph), and the driver and all passengers must wear seatbelts. There are fuel stations in all major towns and most rural ones. It's advisable to fill up whenever you have the opportunity.

Self-drive is a popular option for visitors who like the freedom to travel when and where they please. There are some rules it's important to follow. Firstly, choose a reputable car-hire firm with a modern fleet of vehicles and countrywide back-up support. The **Car Rental Association of Namibia** (*Tel: (061) 242 375. www.caran.org*) has most

of the internationally known companies as members. The condition of the car is vital to your safety, so check it carefully. For most of the sights you'll be visiting, a good 2WD saloon car is adequate. Punctures are common on gravel roads so make sure there are two spare tyres. To go off the beaten track, a 4WD is needed (and experience of driving one).

Read the small print of your hire agreement very carefully, particularly the sections on insurance and collision damage waiver (CDW). The excess you have to pay in the event of an accident can be very high.

Most accidents happen on gravel roads, because people drive too fast. Tempting though it may be, never go above 80kph (50mph). The safest speed on gravel is 60–70kph (35–45mph). The gravel surface hides dips, sandy patches and potholes, while skidding on corners happens all too easily. Be aware

A termite mound in the desert

that blind rises are often followed by slight bends.

Always slow down in the face of oncoming vehicles. Flying stones damage windscreens and you can't see what's ahead in the cloud of dust. If you want to stop to take photographs, park off to the side of the road. Never drive at night, when animals and people can appear from nowhere. During the day, too, keep a wary eye out for farm and wild animals that often stay close to the highway. They may suddenly decide they need to cross the road.

By coach

Intercape Mainliner operates luxury coaches on long-distance routes, covering a vast network of cities and major towns throughout southern Africa. In Namibia it covers most main centres on the route north from South Africa via Windhoek, right up through the Caprivi Strip to Victoria Falls in Zambia. It also has a service to Swakopmund and Walvis Bay. The air-conditioned coaches are comfortable,

have reclining seats, an on-board toilet, audio and video entertainment, and refreshments are available.
Intercape Mainliner. Tel: (021) 380 4400. www.intercape.co.za

By organised tour

A wide range of tours is available, from those covering the highlights of the north or south in a week or two to special-interest safaris for wildlife, birding and photography enthusiasts. Transport can range from big coaches (generally not ideal) to minibuses, 4WD safari vehicles to small planes. There's a huge range of accommodation choices, and new lodges, guest farms and quality campsites are opening all the time. The best tour operators know the country well. Namibia is not a cheap destination, but if you choose a knowledgeable travel company you'll find the country can offer good value for money.

People with disabilities may find an organised tour a suitable way of travelling. Namibians are extremely helpful people and will go out of their way to assist visitors. It's important to ensure that the tour company is aware of your needs and that suitable hotel rooms are booked.

By taxi

Taxis are plentiful and inexpensive in Windhoek and Swakopmund and available in all the main towns. Hail them in the street or ask the hotel or restaurant to call one for you.

By train

Except for the luxury **Desert Express**, rail travel in Namibia is not geared for tourism. Trains are dedicated to freight rather than passengers, they are very slow and the network is limited. Few visitors use them. Mostly they run overnight and have many stops (usually noisy, given they are freight trains). Passenger carriages have airline-type seating, videos are often shown and most services have vending machines for drinks and snacks. The Starline passenger service is operated by **Transnamib**. It's a cheap way to travel and you do get to meet local people.

The Desert Express, however, is a different matter. On its overnight journey between Windhoek and the coast, this stylish train stops for a late-afternoon game drive, then to do some stargazing before a quiet night's sleep. There's an after-breakfast walk among the dunes before arriving in Swakopmund. The reverse route to Windhoek includes sundowners in the Kahn River Valley and a morning visit to a game farm to see lions being fed. The train is air-conditioned, the food is excellent and the 24 compartments, all with en-suite facilities, are small but cleverly designed. It operates year-round from Windhoek on Fridays and Swakopmund on Saturdays.

Desert Express. Tel: (061) 298 2600.
www.desertexpress.com.na
Transnamib. Tel: (061) 298 2175.
www.transnamib.com.na

A vintage steam train preparing to depart from Swakopmund station

Accommodation

From luxury lodges with spas to backpacker hostels and everything in between, Namibia offers its visitors a tremendous choice of accommodation options. What links them all is the charm, friendliness and hospitality of the people who manage and staff them. The Namibia Tourism Board requires every establishment to be graded and registered, which keeps the quality high.

The **Hospitality Association of Namibia (HAN)** *has a useful website listing a wide range of accommodation establishments.* www.hannamibia.com

Bed and breakfast
From farm-stays to city homes, the B&B concept is catching on in Namibia. See the website *www.bed-breakfast-namibia.com*

Camping sites
Camping is such a popular activity in Namibia that there's a huge number of sites to be found all over the country, including beachside up the coast from Swakopmund, on farms, near lakes, on communal conservancy land and in all the national parks. They range from sites with basic facilities to smart versions with all mod cons, including self-catering rooms, even chalets with kitchens. For families on a budget, camping is a great way to see Namibia.

All the camping gear can be bought or hired in Windhoek and Swakopmund. Pre-arrange your requirements if you are hiring. Hire car companies also rent out vehicles fully equipped with everything needed for a camping holiday. They should be booked well in advance of your arrival in Namibia.

Some of the most interesting campsites are on conservancies, rural communal land that is sustainably managed to allow wildlife and people to coexist and to link tourism with community development. For example, the Aba-Huab Campsite near the rock art and desert elephants of Twyfelfontein has sites with fireplaces for *braais* (barbecues), ablution blocks with hot showers and flush toilets, a restaurant and bar, and often puts on performances of traditional singing and dancing.

Camps
Small luxury camps are the upmarket version of camping. Less expensive than lodges, they offer room-sized tents with

en-suite shower/toilet. The tents are usually on raised platforms and may have a veranda. Often in wilderness areas, they are likely to have a small swimming pool, dining room and bar, serve excellent food and offer activities such as game drives and bush walks.

Guest farms

As farming becomes an ever more difficult occupation, many farming families have turned to offering guest accommodation. Others have abandoned livestock farming and stocked their land with game.

Guest farms are working farms where activities such as hiking and horse riding are combined with good country food and friendly hosts happy to share their knowledge of the land. A Namibian farm is likely to be around 10,000ha (24,710 acres) of uncultivated bush and may support some springbok, oryx and other small game.

Game farms or ranches will have been stocked with such wild animals as elephant, black rhino, lion, possibly leopard and cheetah, plus several varieties of antelope, so the main activities of a stay on one will be game-viewing drives and guided bush walks. Both guest farms and game farms are highly likely to have a swimming pool.

Guesthouses

Smaller than the average hotel, larger than the usual B&B, guesthouses tend to provide en-suite, twin-bedded rooms, a small pool, a good breakfast but no restaurant. Some in Windhoek and Swakopmund, however, could best be described as 'boutique hotels', having attractive en-suite rooms, a pool, bar and a good restaurant. Guesthouses are located mainly in Namibia's central and southern regions.

All the rooms at the Lüderitz Nest Hotel have sea views

Hotels

Windhoek and Swakopmund have the biggest choice and range of hotels, but every medium-sized town in the country will have at least one small hotel with a restaurant and bar. Under the Namibia Tourism Board grading system, a hotel must have 20 or more en-suite guest rooms and a hotel pension between 10 and 20 such rooms. 'Hotels' fall within municipal areas, 'lodges' don't.

Being the capital city, Windhoek can offer big hotels of international standard with bars, restaurants, public areas, a swimming pool, gym, conference facilities and car parking.

Lodges

Namibia excels in luxury lodges, some so special you feel you never want to leave. They are invariably set in amazing locations, so the views as well as the décor, design, food, service and facilities are all part of the experience.

Depending on its location, each lodge offers a range of activities, which may include game drives, guided nature walks, horse riding, flights in hot-air balloons, Bushman trails, quad biking, dune-buggy excursions, boating and fishing trips and visits to local communities.

All the lodges have swimming pools, of varying sizes. 'Horizon' pools are exactly that – nothing but Africa between you and the horizon. Some lodges have individual plunge pools alongside each room.

Lodges with a spa and wellness centre offer a range of massages and treatments at prices that seem extremely reasonable to European and North American visitors. After a long day on the road, a relaxing massage in luxurious surroundings

Cañon Lodge is a former farmhouse with a fascinating history

The ultra-comfortable rondavels at Okonjima Bush Lodge are stylishly designed and decorated

with a view out over the bush or desert is a fine experience.

No two lodges are alike. Taking inspiration from the landscape and culture, each one is individually designed and usually built from local materials to blend in beautifully with the surroundings. Accommodation can range from large tented rooms for the 'Out of Africa' feel to thatched *rondavels* (circular bungalows) and chalets. Some lodges are big enough to accommodate large tour groups, while others may have under a dozen rooms.

Meals match the quality and style of the accommodation. Quite how the freshest of ingredients reach the deepest bush or the remotest desert remains a mystery to guests. To wake up to a breakfast table laden with exotic fruits and home-baked breads, jugs brim-full with juices, big bowls of creamy yoghurt and platters of cold meats and cheeses – and then be asked how you'd like your eggs cooked for the 'full' breakfast – seems little short of a miracle. Likewise the four-course, set menu, silver-service dinners that would put many a 5-star city restaurant to the test. The logistics must be a nightmare, but there's never a hint of it.

Staying at a luxury lodge will never be an inexpensive option, but the experience is memorable.

Namibia Wildlife Resorts (NWR)

NWR manages the 12 government-owned resorts in Namibia's national parks and game reserves. In the past they have been inexpensive and fairly basic, but the complete refurbishment of the three rest camps in the Etosha National Park has put them on another level. The design and quality of the accommodation there is excellent, if no longer cheap.

Food and drink

Meat-lovers will be in their element in Namibia, where barbecues are a way of life. Fish appears on many menus, and seafood, in season, at the coast. Much of the fresh produce is imported from neighbouring South Africa, which has given Namibia many of its local dishes plus a taste for wine. Germany, too, has influenced the cuisine and beer is very popular here.

A *braai* (barbecue) is the favoured way of cooking for the family and entertaining friends. Steaks, chops and *sosaties* (kebabs) sizzle alongside spicy *boerewors* ('farmers' sausage'), baked potatoes and grilled vegetables. Every picnic spot and campsite has its *braai* pits, and whether you're in the desert, bush or at the beach, the distinctive aroma of a *braai* wafts through the air to tantalise the taste buds.

The traditional African cast-iron cooking pot known as a *potjie* (pronounced 'poyt-kee') stands sturdily on three legs, sits on the open fire and gives its name to the great stews (*potjiekos*) that are made in it. A variety of vegetables and meat or chicken are placed in layers, stock and seasonings added, then the pot is left to simmer gently for hours. *Potjiekos* are served with rice or *pap*, a stiff maize-meal porridge that's the staple diet for most black Namibians and enjoyed by everyone, especially when served with lashings of gravy.

Eating *biltong*, thin slices of savoury dried meat, is a way of life alongside

drinking beer and watching sport. Usually made from beef, but also kudu, eland or ostrich, it is sold everywhere.

Namibia's cattle, sheep and goats are raised on savannah grasses and shrubs, free from hormones and antibiotics. Likewise the game, such as ostrich, springbok and oryx (or gemsbok), that appears on many menus. Restaurants serve a lot of meat and steakhouses are very popular. Servings are invariably large.

Seasonal specialities worth sampling include Swakopmund green asparagus, rare Kalahari truffles and chewy, sun-dried *mopane* worms fried with spices as a snack or served with *pap*.

When in Lüderitz, feast on its famed rock lobsters. Swakopmund and Walvis Bay are known for their oysters. Restaurants at the coast serve particularly good fish and seafood.

Vegetarians are catered for, though not exactly overwhelmed with choice. Given advance notice, most chefs at upmarket lodges will happily produce

Food and drink

Fresh local ingredients feature on Namibian menus

special dishes for vegetarians. In fact these lodges, despite their out-of-the-way locations and long distances from food sources, present some of the best cuisine to be found in Namibia.

Supermarkets in big towns are a good source of fresh fruit and vegetables. They are the cheapest place to buy bottled water for journeys, also ice for the coolbox. They sell wine and beer, but you'll have to go to the bottle store (*drankwinkel* in Afrikaans) for anything stronger. Alcohol is only sold until 5pm on weekdays, 1pm on Saturdays and never on Sundays.

Beer is the favourite local drink, brewed by Nambrew following a law issued in 1516 in Bavaria. Look for the Windhoek and Hansa brands. Good wines are imported from South Africa. For a long, non-alcoholic drink ask for a 'rock shandy'. A mix of lemonade, soda water and dashes of Angostura bitters, it is very refreshing.

Service in hotels and restaurants is usually very good, but wages are very low so a tip of about ten per cent will be welcomed. At lodges where meals and accommodation are included in the price, there's always a staff tip box in reception.

Entertainment

Music plays a big role in Namibian life and several superb choirs have won acclaim worldwide. From formal concerts to impromptu performances of traditional singing, dancing and drumming, music reflects the many different groups that coexist in the country. Windhoek is the centre of a lively cultural scene, many towns have annual festivals and summer holidays at the coast are a time for partying.

Windhoek may not be known for its wild nightlife but it has the best cultural scene in the country. The most popular venue is the Warehouse Theatre, which has an eclectic mix of African and European sounds and hosts some of the best musicians in southern Africa. There's a different event every night, mainly music but live theatre and poetry readings, too. The bar there opens until late.

The National Theatre of Namibia (NTN) is the place to go for concerts, opera, ballet and contemporary dance as well as live theatre productions and the film festival. The Windhoek Symphony Orchestra performs there and ballet and plays are often presented in collaboration with South African performing arts councils and international organisations.

Programmes at the University of Namibia's Performing Arts Department span music recitals, art, drama, ballet and experimental theatre, while the College for the Arts has art exhibitions and performances by its Chamber Orchestra. The Franco-Namibian Cultural Centre (FNCC) often hosts concerts, art exhibitions, lectures and events and shows films in its small cinema.

As well as the changing exhibitions at the National Art Gallery of Namibia (NAGN) there are usually several art exhibitions going on around town at galleries and in shopping malls. The Bank Windhoek Omba Gallery in the Crafts Centre is a good source of work by both African and European artists.

Walalapo Windhoek is a free monthly listings guide to what's on in the capital. It's available at the tourist information centres and in many restaurants and hotels.

The Swakopmund Hotel and Entertainment Centre, which has a big casino, is the main venue at the coast for music. Swakopmund's many galleries have changing exhibitions featuring work by Namibian artists.

Bars and nightlife

There's no equivalent of the British pub, so when Namibians want to relax over a drink they choose bars at hotels and restaurants. Windhoek and Swakopmund have a few nightclubs but it is a rapidly changing scene. Venues go in and out of fashion, so you need to ask around to find the current 'in' and safe place to go. If you want to experience some of the bars or clubs in a township, get a local to take you or join one of the organised township tours that operate to Katutura in Windhoek (*see p37*) and to Mondesa in Swakopmund (*see p89*).

Choirs

There's a long tradition of choral singing in Namibia, and if you get the opportunity to hear a concert, don't miss it. Among the most famous names are the University of Namibia's UNAM Choir, which tours the world and has recorded some excellent CDs, Namibia's National Youth Choir, and Cantate Audire, a Windhoek choir that also travels abroad and has won international awards. At the coast, listen out for the Mascato Coastal Youth Choir and Walvis Bay Marimba Band.

Cinema

Windhoek has a five-screen multiplex cinema in the big Maerua Park Mall shopping centre. Swakopmund's three-screen cinema is on the pedestrian Brauhaus Arcade. Both show international releases and ticket prices seem low compared with European prices. There are often reductions for afternoon screenings. Drinks and snacks are available.

The Atlanta Cinema in Swakopmund

Shopping

If you love crafts then you may find your luggage bulging when you carry all your treasures home. Woodcarvings and hand-woven baskets are favourite buys. Jewellery, however, fits into small spaces. Diamonds from the coast near Lüderitz and gemstones mined in Damaraland and the north are fashioned into beautiful jewellery by talented local designers in Windhoek and Swakopmund.

Windhoek and Swakopmund are Namibia's major shopping centres but wherever you travel, particularly in the northern half of the country, you will find crafts on sale. Some of the crafts markets and curio shops sell goods from many different African countries, so to be sure you are buying something truly Namibian, do ask if it is locally made.

Shopping to make a difference

Often you will hear that your chosen purchase has been made by one of the many craft projects and cooperatives that are successfully being formed around the country and bring work and an income to marginalised rural women. Names to look out for include the **Penduka** project in Katutura, Windhoek (*see p38*), **People in Need Namibia**, based in Keetmanshoop (*Wake Centre, Tseib Ave. Tel: (063) 224 364. Open: Mon–Fri 8am–5pm*) and producing delightful toy animals, dolls and beaded bags, and the **Anin** project in the Kalahari. Nama

women are skilled embroiderers and Anin ('birds' in Nama) employs around 300 rural women to make superb bed and table linen that has a modern yet classic feel.

Traditional crafts

The baskets that have always been woven for domestic use are now sought-after craft items. Making them to sell is providing a lifeline for many women in rural northern Namibia. They are beautifully constructed from the leaves of the makalani palm (*Hyphaene petersiana*), using the coil technique. Symbolic geometric patterns in shades of brown, purple or yellow, created by boiling the leaves, bark and roots of various shrubs and trees, are often woven into the mats and baskets. The **Namibia Mbangura Woodcarvers** have a huge outdoor market at Okahandja, 70km (44 miles) north of Windhoek. The sheer number of the stalls and variety of the carvings can seem overwhelming, but it's an essential stop on the road between Windhoek and the Etosha National Park and it's open pretty much all the time.

Where to buy what
Lüderitz
Sandrose Boutique
Unusual gift items for the home, sourced mainly from Namibia and South Africa.
15 Bismarck St. Tel: (063) 203 686.

Swakopmund
African Curiotique
Stylish crafts and jewellery, decorated ostrich eggs, textiles, glassware and ornaments.
Nedbank Arcade. Tel: (064) 461 062.

Buy Namibian and support talented local craftspeople

African Kirikara
Sells artefacts, furnishings, baskets, ceramics and jewellery from all over Africa but has a fine selection of Namibian-made crafts, too. They have studios on Farm Kiripotib ('the place where the lion comes to drink') in the Kalahari, where innovative jewellery is designed and hand-woven karakul wool carpets are made.
Ankerplatz, Sam Nujoma Ave.
Tel: (064) 463 146. www.kirikara.com

Art Africa Craft
A great selection of rural crafts, township art, pottery and ethnic jewellery. Their **Tribal Art** shop has woven baskets, textiles, carvings, pots and ceramics from all over Africa.
Crafts, Shop 6, The Arcade.
Tel: (064) 404 024.
Tribal Art, 6 Hendrik Witbooi St.
Tel: (064) 463 454.

Casa Anin
The finest-quality bed linen, cushion covers and tablemats all hand-embroidered. African classics.
Nedbank Arcade. Tel: (064) 405 910.
www.anin.com.na

Die Muschel
A big selection of literature on Namibia, as well as international fiction and non-fiction. The children's section is excellent. There's an art gallery upstairs.
Nedbank Arcade. Tel: (064) 402 874.

Karakulia Weavers
Hand-woven rugs and wall hangings in designs that include landscapes, animal scenes and contemporary images. To see how they are made, take a tour of

Handwoven baskets in a multitude of designs, crafted in northern Namibia

their workshop. You can commission a rug to be woven to your own design and reliably shipped back home.
Shop: Brauhaus Arcade.
Workshop and studio: 2 Rakotoka St.
Tel: (064) 461 415. www.karakulia.com.na

Namibian Jewellers and Arts
Goldsmith Michael Engelhard takes inspiration from the Namib Desert.
55 Sam Nujoma Ave. Tel: 081 298 8882.

Peter's Antiques
Packed with Africana, together with Namibian carvings, Bushman ostrich-shell jewellery and musical instruments, this shop is a treasure trove and its owner is very knowledgeable.
24 Tobias Hainyeko St. Tel: (064) 405 624.

Zebra Crossin'
Modern jewellery in silver and a lovely selection of gifts.
Daniel Tjongarero St.
Tel: (064) 403 888.

Windhoek
You should be able to find everything you need in Windhoek. On Independence Avenue, Town Square Centre, the Levinson Arcade and the Gustav Voigts Centre under the Kalahari Sands Hotel, you'll find packed-in shops and boutiques selling everything from fashion to gourmet foods, homeware and gifts.

For an outdoor display of crafts and curios look in Post Street Mall, where traders lay out their wares among the shops and cafés. Also visit the sellers of carvings, baskets and bead jewellery who gather on the pavement on the corner of Independence Avenue and Fidel Castro Street, opposite Zoo Park.

Adrian & Meyer
Fine craftsmanship using Namibian gold and gemstones in designs that are modern classics.
250 Independence Ave. Tel: (061) 236 100.

Adrian & Meyer – The Trend Shop

The trendy version of the main shop on Independence Avenue.
Shop 3A, Maerua Mall.
Tel: (061) 223 635.
www.adrian-meyer-jewellers.com.na

Adventure Camping Hire and Sales

Comprehensive range, from roof tents and portable toilets to kitchen boxes and camping chairs, available to hire. Contact them well in advance so your pack is ready for collection when you arrive.
74 Laurent Desiré Kabila St.
Tel: (061) 242 478.

Bushman Art Gallery

Curios, souvenirs and gifts, including books, T-shirts, leather goods, gemstones and tribal art and masks.
Erkraths Building, 187 Independence Ave. Tel: (061) 228 828.

House of Gems

Particularly famed for tourmaline, its range of gemstones mined in Namibia is outstanding. Here you can watch the finest stones being sorted, cut and faceted.
131 Werner List St. Tel: (061) 225 202.

Nakara

Stylish, high-quality coats and jackets fashioned from Namibian karakul leathers. Smart handbags, too.
165 Independence Ave. Tel: (061) 224 209.

Namibia Crafts Centre

A superb source of traditional crafts from all over Namibia. Many of the cooperatives are represented here, so you can be sure your purchases are fairly traded.
40 Tal St. Tel: (061) 242 222.

Safariland

With a big selection of safari gear and bushwear, this is the place to get kitted out for travelling around Namibia.
Kalahari Sands Hotel (street level).
Tel: (061) 235 941.

The New Bookcellar

Has a good selection of books on Namibia, also maps and guides.
Carl List Haus, Fidel Castro St.
Tel: (061) 231 615.

Animal carvings at the outdoor crafts market in Windhoek

Sport and leisure

Namibians are united in their love of sport as the sunny, dry climate makes Namibia an outdoorsy, sporty kind of country. It is also getting a name for adrenalin activities, especially at the coast where sand boarding and quad biking are hugely popular. Here you can play golf on sandy greens, fish for big catches, go horse riding in the desert or skydiving over dunes.

Football and rugby fill the hearts of the sport-loving Namibians who follow their teams with fervour and never miss an opportunity to watch or talk about their favourite subject. Windhoek's Independence Stadium holds 25,000 people and the Katutura Soccer Stadium can pack in 15,000. For leisure, anglers flock to the coast over the summer holidays.

Ballooning

Surely the most romantic and beautiful way to travel. Soaring peacefully above the desert is a stunning way to experience the beauty of Sossusvlei (*see Directory, p164*).

Canoeing

Four- and six-day canoeing trips down the Orange River are available (*www.wildthing.co.za*), and, unlike most African rivers, there's nothing dangerous lurking in the water.

Fishing

Beach and offshore fishing from Walvis Bay and up into the Skeleton Coast National Park brings in good catches of kabeljou, steenbras, blacktail, barbel and galjoen. Of the various shark species, gully shark and bronze whaler shark are most frequently caught, but the copper shark is the big challenge. Many companies offer fishing trips from Walvis Bay and Swakopmund. The best time of the year for ocean fishing is November to March. On fishing safaris, environmentally aware companies support a catch-and-release policy.

Up in the far northeast, rapacious tiger fish are the attraction for sport fishing fans on the Zambezi River. June to December, when the river subsides, is the best time.

Inland, lakes and dams provide good freshwater fishing. The Hardap Dam near Mariental has been stocked with tilapia, small-mouth yellowfish, mudfish, catfish and common carp. The Von Bach Dam north of Windhoek has

large-mouthed bass, blue kurper, carp and barbel. Both dams are also favoured sites for waterskiing and sailing.
www.namibweb.com/fishinginfo.html

Golf

On the southern edge of the capital close to Eros airport, the Windhoek Golf and Country Club has an 18-hole course on lush grass fairways that is highly rated (*see Directory, p160*). Caddies and motorised caddy carts are available, the practice range is floodlit and there are two resident pros.

Against a stunning backdrop of red dunes and date palm trees, Rossmund Golf Course near Swakopmund is one of only five 18-hole fully grassed desert courses in the world – but possibly the only one with springbok roaming freely across it (*see Directory, p168*). The first nine holes were designed by Robert Trent-Jones, the second nine holes by South African golfer Bill Kerr.

Golf clubs can be hired at both of these courses.

There's a novel nine-hole desert golf course at Walvis Bay (*Tel: (081) 271 6950*). Here the greens and tees have grass, the fairways consist of a clay composite and players tee up on the fairways. North of Swakopmund, the challenging nine-hole course at Henties

Hiking the Fish River Canyon Trail is challenging but rewarding

Bay (*Tel: (064) 500 393*) has well-tended green islands dotting sandy fairways along an old riverbed.

For those who really like a challenge, there's a rough and tough course at Lüderitz. It has no grass and can only be played from March to October. The rest of the year is just too windy.

Hiking

Namibia has some fantastic trails for serious hikers. The 'big ones' are the five-day 85km-long (53 mile) Fish River Canyon Trail (*see p48*), open only between mid-April and mid-September, and the eight-day, 120km (75 mile) Namib-Naukluft Hiking Trail. Both are tough, pass through spectacular scenery and are very rewarding.

Three-day hikes include the guided Ugab Hiking Trail for 50km (31 miles) along the Skeleton Coast and the 34km (21 mile) Feral Horse Hiking Trail, which traverses the Aus mountains and is named after the wild horses that roam the desert plains west of **Klein-Aus Vista** (*Tel: (063) 258 021. www.namibhorses.com*).

The Olive Trail and the more demanding Waterkloof Trail are two hikes in the Naukluft section of the Namib-Naukluft National Park that can be completed in a day. The Namib section of the park offers a three-hour Rock Sculpture Trail and the Tinkas Nature Walk that takes around five hours.

Contact **Namibia Wildlife Resorts**

(Tel: (061) 285 7200. www.nwr.com.na) for bookings and information on hikes in all the national parks.

Horse riding

For accomplished riders there are long trails, one that starts in the Khomas Hochland near Windhoek and finishes 400km (almost 250 miles) later on the beach at Swakopmund, and another of 250km (155 miles) through Damaraland that takes in Twyfelfontein rock paintings and the Aba-Huab River, favoured by desert elephant. Many guest farms and lodges offer short rides on their property. **Grootberg Lodge** has sunset rides that can be enjoyed even by inexperienced riders. From **Cañon Lodge** you can ride for a few hours or several days.

See Directory for listings.

Mountain biking

Organised mountain biking has taken off in a big way in Namibia. The

Swakopmund is famed for adrenalin sports

rugged, mountainous escarpment of the central plateau in particular offers plenty of opportunities for exhilarating and tough challenges.
www.mountainbikenamibia.com

Paragliding

The fresh southwesterly winds across the dunes south of Swakopmund offer ideal 'lift' and the views from on high are amazing.
See Directory for listings.

Quad biking

A top desert experience, but destructive to the environment, so do go on one of the guided trips organised by a reputable operator. Three areas in the dunes between Swakopmund and Walvis Bay have been designated for use by quad bikes and off-road vehicles.
See Directory for listings.

Rock climbing

Rising above the plains in southern Damaraland, the 1,728m (5,670ft) Spitzkoppe is Namibia's top rock-climbing destination. As well as the natural rock climbing areas, there are some routes secured with bolts, making them suitable for sport climbing. The Erongo Mountains in the same area also offer climbing challenges.
Windhoek Mountain Club.
Tel: (061) 241 829.

Sand boarding

Buffeted by southwest winds and with altitudes of up to 120m (394ft), sand

Spitzkoppe is popular with rock climbers

boarders are said to be able to reach speeds of 80kph (50mph) on the slopes and slip faces of the high dunes south of Swakopmund. Tuition is provided and, depending on your skills, sand boarding can be done standing up or lying down on the board.
See Directory for listings.

Skydiving

The Swakopmund Skydiving Club offers courses (*www.skydiveswakop.com.na*). You can also do tandem skydives.

Spas

Several of the lodges in the Leading Lodges of Africa group have beautifully appointed spas, some with wilderness views, offering blissful treatments. They are on the edge of the Etosha National Park, in the desert near Sossusvlei and on the Okavango River up in Caprivi. There's also a Wellness Village in the GocheGanas Nature Reserve 29km (18 miles) southeast of Windhoek, which is wheelchair accessible.
See Directory for listings.

Children

Forget The Lion King, *this is the real thing. Visit the Etosha National Park in the dry season, and the sight of so many animals at the waterholes will have everyone from tots to teens (and the grown-ups) captivated. Children are welcomed in Namibia, and with so much wildlife and adventure on offer they'll have the time of their lives.*

Accommodation

There are campsites everywhere that are perfect for families. Namibians love camping and are friendly people, so it's a good way for children to make new friends. If you choose community-run sites on conservancy land, they'll have the opportunity of learning about different cultures, too.

Hotels and lodges often have special rates for children. Namibia Wildlife Resorts (NWR), which manages the resorts in all the national parks and reserves, gives a 50 per cent discount for children aged six to twelve, while under-sixes stay free of charge. Also, they only charge adults the park entry fees. Under-16s in the vehicle get free park entry.

Namibia is a family-friendly country and many of the accommodation options have specific family rooms or adjoining rooms that are good if there's a big gap in the children's ages. There are plenty of family chalets or bungalows, especially in the parks and lakeside resorts. Not all lodges are suitable for young children, often because they are sited among rocks or perhaps on the edge of a canyon. These clearly state the ages accepted, which may be above eight or twelve.

Eating and shopping

Supermarkets in the main towns are very well stocked, both with fresh and canned food and all the essentials needed by babies, young children and teenagers. Babycare products are also available in pharmacies.

TRAVEL AND SUN ESSENTIALS

Long car journeys can be boring, so pack plenty of books and games. Try focusing attention on spotting springbok, ostriches and other wildlife.

The sun is strong in Namibia, sunburn happens swiftly and using a high-factor sunscreen is essential. So is wearing a hat. Always carry plenty of bottled water. The excellent fruit juices are a good alternative to fizzy drinks.

Many restaurants have a children's menu and most will do smaller portions of adult servings (which are generally huge). Should your little ones tire of the meat and chicken dishes that dominate Namibian menus, there are plenty of pasta and pizza alternatives, as well as numerous fast-food outlets.

Seaside treats

The sea is too cold for swimming and rip tides are dangerous, but Swakopmund's sandy Palm Beach is sheltered and popular with local families. There's a grassy park and children's playground with swings right beside it and the big municipal swimming pool is close by as well.

Swakopmund is a good town for children. As well as the **National Marine Aquarium** with a walk-through tunnel in a big tank and touch pools (*see pp82–3*), it has the **Kristall Galerie** housing the biggest crystal cluster in the world (*see p82*) and a **Living Desert Snake Park** in an old mining railway station, where they feed the snakes at 10am on Saturdays (*Otavi Bahnhof, Sam Nujoma Ave, Swakopmund. Tel: (064) 405 100. Open: Mon–Fri 8.30am–5pm, Sat 8.30am–1pm. Admission charge*).

Down the road in Walvis Bay, dolphin-watching cruises are a big hit. Seals come out of the water to board the boats and don't at all mind being stroked and fed. Horse- and camel-riding in the desert make interesting experiences. Sand boarding and quad biking in the towering sand dunes should give teens a thrill, and instruction and safety equipment are supplied (*see Directory for listings*).

A children's playground by the beach at Swakopmund

Essentials

Arriving and departing
Arriving by air
Air Namibia has direct flights to Windhoek from London (Gatwick) and Frankfurt. The alternative is to fly to South Africa and get a connecting flight to Windhoek. Many airlines have routes to Johannesburg or Cape Town, including British Airways, South African Airways and Virgin. Qantas flies from Australia and Cathay Pacific from the Far East.

Windhoek's modern, clean and well-organised Hosea Kutako International Airport is 42km (26 miles) east of the city centre. Taxis and shuttle services are available into town. The journey time is about 30 minutes.

Departing by air
There is no departure tax. At the airport you will need to complete a departure form before going through passport control. If you are claiming back VAT (*see p153*) make sure you have presented your purchases at the Customs desk and received a stamped VAT Refund form before getting the exit stamp on your passport. The refund is paid in the departure lounge (queues can be lengthy, so allow time for this).

By land
Six border posts are in operation between South Africa and Namibia, four with Botswana, three with Angola and one with Zambia. The Trans-Kalahari Highway from Gauteng in South Africa, the Trans-Caprivi Highway in the north and the N7 from Cape Town are all good asphalt-surfaced roads.

If you are taking your own car into Namibia, you need to show documentary proof of ownership such as the registration document. If you are driving a hire car in from South Africa, the hire company should provide you with the necessary paperwork.

Customs
Anyone over the age of 18 is allowed to import free of tax 400 cigarettes or 50 cigars or 250g of tobacco; 2 litres of wine and 1 litre of spirits; 50ml of perfume and 250ml of eau de toilette; gifts to the value of N$50,000 (including the value of imported duty-free items).

Electricity
The power supply in Namibia is 220V AC and 50Hz. Plugs with three round pins are used, as in South Africa. Adaptors for foreign appliances may be found in Windhoek and Swakopmund. Generators are widely used to supply electricity in country properties.

Internet
More and more internet cafés are opening up around the country and the number of Wi-Fi hotspots is increasing.

Hotels usually have internet facilities, but they can be pricey.

Money

The currency is the Namibian Dollar (N$), divided into 100 cents. Notes are in denominations of N$200, N$100, N$50, N$20 and N$10. Coins come in amounts of N$5, N$1, 50 cents, 10 cents and 5 cents. You can use both the South African Rand and N$ in Namibia, but the Namibian Dollar cannot be used in South Africa.

Traveller's cheques and cash can be exchanged at banks in urban centres and at Windhoek airport. Having the former issued in South African Rand makes them easier to cash and cuts down on commission charges.

Major credit cards are widely accepted in Namibia, particularly VISA and MasterCard, both in shops and at cash machines (ATMs). These latter are widespread. It's essential to have cash in rural areas and at all petrol stations.

Opening hours

Shopping hours in big towns are generally Mon–Fri 9am–5pm, Sat 9am–1pm. Some shops close at lunchtime. Few open on Sunday, although some bigger supermarkets open Sun 11am–1pm & 4–7pm.
Office hours are Mon–Fri 8am–5pm, with a one-hour lunch break.
Banking hours are Mon–Fri 9am–3.30pm, Sat 8am–12.30pm.
Most petrol stations on main roads are open 24 hours.

Passports and visas

All visitors require a passport valid for at least six months beyond the intended stay. An entry visa is not required by nationals of EU countries, Australia, New Zealand, the USA, Canada or South Africa for stays of up to 90 days. However, it is always worth checking current requirements with the Namibian Embassy or Consulate in your home country before you travel (*http://namibia.embassy-uk.co.uk*).

Pharmacies

Pharmacies in all the big towns are well stocked, though the brand names may not be familiar, so bringing a list of the ingredients of any prescription medicine you may need can be a good idea – your doctor should be able to provide this. The pharmacists are generally very helpful.

Post

Post offices open Mon–Fri 8am–4.30pm, Sat 8am–noon. Airmail to Europe takes about two weeks, surface mail about three months.

Public holidays

1 January	New Year's Day
21 March	Independence Day
March/April (dates vary)	Good Friday, Easter Monday
1 May	Workers Day
4 May	Cassinga Day
May (dates vary)	Ascension Day
25 May	Africa Day
26 August	Heroes Day

10 December	Women's Day
25 December	Christmas Day
26 December	Family Day

Although not public holidays, special events are usually organised on **9 February** (Constitution Day) and **24 October** (United Nations Day).

Smoking

There is no law against smoking in public places at the time of writing, but most restaurants have designated smoking and non-smoking areas.

Suggested reading and media
Books

Most of the best books on the country are to be found when you're in Namibia. Some to look out for are:
Namibia, A Visual Celebration by Jéan du Plessis, Struik, 2007. Large-format book with superb images of Namibia's landscapes.
A Photographic Guide to the Birds of Namibia by Ian and Jackie Sinclair, Struik 2003. Useful paperback to have when you're travelling.
A Drink of Dry Land by Julienne du Toit and Chris Marais, Struik 2006. Very readable accounts of a journalist couple's journey through Namibia.
The Namib: Natural History of an Ancient Desert by Dr Mary Seely, Shell Namibia, 2004. The most authoritative book on the Namib, its dunes, plants and wildlife.
The Skeleton Coast by Amy Schoeman, Struik, 2003. The definitive, fully illustrated guide to this mysterious coastal wilderness.
The Sheltering Desert by Henno Martin, A D Donker, 1988. How two German geologists survived in the Kuiseb Canyon during World War II.

History and politics
Africa: A Biography of the Continent by John Reader, Penguin Books, 1997. Puts Namibian history into context.
Rivers of Blood, Rivers of Gold: Europe's Conflict with Tribal Peoples by Mark Cocker, Jonathan Cape, 1998. Contains a big section on the German campaign in South West Africa and a detailed account of the 1904–7 war.
The Price of Freedom by Ellen Ndeshi Namhila, New Namibia Books, 1997. A young woman's autobiographical account of her 19 years in exile.

Media
The state-owned Namibian Broadcasting Corporation (NBC) broadcasts an English radio service and one television channel (NBC TV). South African M-Net channels are widely available.

Namibia's media publishes and broadcasts in English, Afrikaans, German and indigenous languages. There are daily newspapers in English, Afrikaans (*Die Republikein*) and German (*Allgemeine Zeitung*). The main English-language publications are:
The Namibia Economist Weekly, published every Friday.

Namibia News Online update of Namibian and world news. *www.namibianews.com*

The Namibian Namibia's biggest-selling independent daily newspaper with comment and opinion columns. *www.namibian.com.na*

New Era Government-owned, reports on community-related issues. Articles are in English and indigenous Namibian languages. *www.newera.com.na*

The Southern Times A regional Sunday newspaper covering Southern African news from an African perspective. *www.southerntimes.com.na*

Tax

VAT is charged on the majority of goods and services at 15 per cent. A 2 per cent 'bed levy' is added to accommodation prices.

Foreign nationals can reclaim VAT on purchases totalling N$250 or more that are to be taken out of the country. Ask for a VAT receipt when buying goods in shops. Leaflets on how to claim VAT back can be found at the airport and in many hotels.

Telephones

The international dialling code for Namibia is 264. GSM mobile (cell phone) coverage is limited but improving all the time. Look for the MTC (Mobile Telecommunications Company) coverage maps or see *www.mtc.com.na*

International calls are very expensive. A cheaper alternative is to buy a Namibian SIM card (you will need to get your phone unlocked before leaving home) and pay-as-you-go top-up cards from a phone shop.

International calls can be made from public phone boxes using phonecards, which can be bought at post offices and supermarkets.

Time

Namibia operates daylight saving, which divides the year into two 'seasons'.

Summertime: GMT+2 hours from the first Sunday in September to the first Sunday in April

Wintertime: GMT+1 hour from the first Sunday in April to the first Sunday in September.

Toilets

Public toilets in restaurants and petrol stations are usually well maintained and free. The 'long drops' in national parks leave much to be desired.

Travellers with disabilities

Namibia isn't the most practical country to travel to if you have a disability. Few buildings have disabled access. Many hotels have ground-floor rooms and some lodges have accommodation that can be easily accessed. Safaris do not usually present too much of a problem as most of the time is spent in the vehicle. It is important to make sure the tour company you are travelling with is aware of your needs, however.

Language

English is the official language in Namibia, but due to the country's years under South African administration, Afrikaans functions as the lingua franca and you are likely to hear it spoken almost everywhere.

Words are generally pronounced the way they are spelt. Afrikaans originated from the language spoken by the early Dutch settlers, and while over the centuries it has evolved and incorporated many words from a variety of sources, it retains the guttural sounds of Dutch and German that do not occur in English, especially the guttural 'g' and the rolled 'r'.

PRONUNCIATION

a	ar as in far, or u as in mum
ai or **aai**	as in tie
d	t as in tart, usually at the end of a word
dt	when ending a word, only the t is pronounced
ee	as in deer
g	a guttural sound, similar to the Scottish ch as in loch. Try saying a rasping k at the back of the throat. This sound is indicated by kh in the pronunciations below
i	eh as in end, or uh as in purse
ie	ee as in seen
j	y as in yes
ô	au as in cause
oo	oo-a
ou	oh as in stone
r	rolled, rr
tj	k as in kick
v	f as in fun
w	v as in vest
y	when used as a vowel, a as in may

NUMBERS

1	een (*e-an*)
2	twee (*tweea*)
3	drie (*dree*)
4	vier (*fear*)
5	vyf (*fayf*)
6	ses (*sayss*)
7	sewe (*sier-ver*)
8	agt (*akht*)
9	nege (*neekher*)
10	tien (*tin*)
20	twintig (*tvuntukh*)
21	een-en-twintig (*e-an-en-tvuntukh*)
50	vyftig (*fayf-takh*)
100	een honderd (*e-an hondert*)
1,000	een duisend (*e-an doisunt*)

DAYS OF THE WEEK

Monday	Maandag (*maan-dtakh*)
Tuesday	Dinsdag (*dins-dtakh*)
Wednesday	Woensdag (*voons-dtakh*)
Thursday	Donderdag (*doonter-dtakh*)
Friday	Vrydag (*fray-dtakh*)
Saturday	Saterdag (*suhter-dtakh*)
Sunday	Sondag (*son-dtakh*)

GREETINGS AND POLITENESS

Hello	Hallo
How are you?	Hoe gaan dit? (*hoo khaan dit?*)
Goodbye	Totsiens (*tawt seens*)
Good morning	Goeiemôre (*khoo-ee-a mawra*)
Good afternoon	Goeiemiddag (*khoo-ee-a mudakh*)
Good evening	Goieinaand (*khoo-ee-a naant*)
Good night	Goeienag (*khoo-ee-a nakh*)
Please	Asseblief (*ah-se-bleef*)
Thank you very much	Baie dankie (*buy-a-donkey*)
Pleased to meet you	Bly te kenne (*blay te k-eh-ne*)
What is your name?	Wat is u naam? (*vat es oo narm?*)
My name is …	My naam is … (*may narm es …*)
Excuse me	Verskoon my (*ferskoo-an may*)
Do you speak English?	Praat u Engels? (*praat oo ingls?*)

EVERYDAY EXPRESSIONS

Yes	Ja (*yar*)
No	Nee (*neah*)
I don't know	Ek weet nie (*ek vee-at nee*)
I am looking for …	Ek soek … (*ek soak …*)
I don't understand	Ek verstaan nie (*ek ferstaan nee*)
Where is the nearest toilet?	Waar is die naaste toilet? (*Var is dee nahste toah-elet?*)
We'd like to see the menu	Ons wil graag die spyskaart sien (*Awns vel kh-rah-kh dee spays-kart seen*)
Good (tasty food)	Lekker (*leh-ker*)
Please bring the bill	Bring asseblief die rekening (*brung asse-bleef die reckunung*)
Tea/coffee/sugar/milk	Tee/koffie/suiker/melk (*teah/kawfee/sayker/melk*)
Wine/beer/water	Wyn/bier/water (*vayn/beerr/varter*)
Cheers!	Gesondheid! (*khusond-hait!*)
Left/right	Links/regs (*lunkts/rrekhs*)
Far/near	Ver/naby (*fairr/narbay*)
Open/closed	Oop/toe (*ooap/too*)
How much does this cost?	Hoeveel kos dit? (*hoofeel cos dit?*)
Yes, I'll buy it	Ja, ek sal dit koop (*yar, ek sal dit koo-arp*)

TIME

What is the time?	Hoe laat is dit? (*hoo laht is dit?*)
Today	Vandag (*vandakh*)
Yesterday	Gister (*khister*)
Tomorrow	Môre (*mawra*)

Emergencies

Crime

Namibia is a low-crime country and generally very safe, but you should still use the same precautions as you would at home or travelling anywhere. Keep separate copies of important documents, including your passport. Most crime is opportunistic, so keep a firm hand on your possessions and, if driving, stow valuables out of sight. Police are visible in Windhoek and Swakopmund and can be safely approached if needed.

Embassies

Australia

There is no Australian Commission in Namibia. The nearest is in South Africa.
Australian High Commission.
292 Orient St, Arcadia, Pretoria,
South Africa. Tel:(+27 12) 423 6000.

British High Commission

116 Robert Mugabe Ave, Windhoek.
Tel: (061) 274 800.

Canada

The nearest Canadian representative is in South Africa.
Canadian High Commission.
1103 Arcadia St, Hatfield, Pretoria.
Tel: (+27 12) 422 3000.

New Zealand

The New Zealand High Commissioner to South Africa is accredited to Namibia.
New Zealand High Commission.
Block C (2nd floor), Hatfield Gardens,
1110 Arcadia St, Hatfield, Pretoria.
Tel: (+27 12) 342 8656.

South African High Commission

Corner Nelson Mandela Ave & Jan
Jonker St, Windhoek.
Tel: (061) 205 7111.

United States Embassy

14 Lossen St, Windhoek.
Tel: (061) 295 8500.

Emergency telephone numbers

Namibia does not have a single number to call in case of emergency. Here are numbers for emergencies in the main centres:

Keetmanshoop (area code 063)

Ambulance and hospital 223 388
Fire 221 211
Police 10111

Lüderitz (area code 063)

Ambulance and hospital 202 466
Police and Fire 202 255

Otjiwarongo (area code 067)

Ambulance 303 734
Hospital 302 2491
Fire 304 444
Police 10111
Medi-Clinic 303 734

Swakopmund (area code 064)

Ambulance and State hospital 410 6000
Fire 410 4111
Police 10111
Cottage Medi-Clinic (private) 412 200

Walvis Bay (area code 064)

Ambulance 209 832
Police 10111
Fire 203 117
State Hospital 216 300
Welwitschia Hospital 209 000

Windhoek (area code 061)

Ambulance and Fire 211 111
Police 10111
Windhoek Central Hospital 203 9111
Medi Clinic Private Hospital 222 687

International SOS organise medical evacuations from anywhere.
Tel: 0800 911 911 (toll free from a land line) or (061) 230 505.

Many lodges are members, covering you while you are staying with them, and some car-hire companies include temporary membership of International SOS in the hire agreement. Serious problems cost serious money. It is very important to have good travel insurance.

Health risks and care

Namibia is generally a very healthy country to visit. Standards of hygiene in good restaurants, lodges, hotels, guesthouses, camps and guest farms are at least as high as in your own country. The main causes of problems are dehydration from the heat, 'traveller's tummy', sunburn and car accidents caused by driving too fast on gravel roads. However, malaria is endemic in northern Namibia and does present a serious health risk, particularly in the rainy season (Dec–Apr). Also be aware that Namibia has one of the highest rates of HIV/AIDS infection in the world.

Tap water in towns and borehole water in remote locations is safe to drink, although you may not always like the taste. Bottled water is widely available and you should always have plenty with you when travelling. Namibia is a hot, dry country and it is easy to get dehydrated. Cover up, wear a hat and always use sunblock or a very high-factor sunscreen. The sun's glare hurts your eyes, so wear good UV-protection sun glasses and bring soothing eye drops. Contact lens wearers may prefer to switch to glasses in the desert. Protect yourself against insect bites with an effective repellent.

Hospitals

The main hospitals are good – note that you will be expected to pay for treatment. There are renowned private hospitals in Windhoek and Otjiwarongo. Doctors and dentists are listed in the telephone book. Pharmacies are well stocked.

Directory

Accommodation price guide

Prices shown are based on a double room per night for two people sharing and include breakfast. Most lodges include dinner in the rate and this is noted under individual listings. Campsite prices do not include breakfast.

★	Under N$750
★★	N$750–1,500
★★★	N$1,500–2,500
★★★★	Over N$2,500

Eating out price guide

Prices are based on an average two-course meal per head, without drinks.

★	Under N$50
★★	N$50–100
★★★	N$100–150
★★★★	Over N$150

WINDHOEK AND CENTRAL NAMIBIA
Windhoek
ACCOMMODATION

Tamboti Guesthouse ★
Friendly B&B guesthouse with 15 rooms, terrace, pool and views of the Khomas Hochland. In a quiet residential area with secure parking, it has wheelchair-accessible rooms. About 15 minutes' walk from the city centre.
9 Kerby St.
Tel: (061) 235 515.

Hotel-Pension Thule ★★
High on a hill with city and mountain views, the palm-tree-flanked Thule is airy, light, peaceful and very modern. It has 14 comfortable rooms (one of the twin-bedded rooms has disabled access) and a good-sized pool. The à la carte restaurant has an adjoining balcony for dining under the stars or a leisurely sunshine breakfast.
1 Gorges St.
Tel: (061) 250 146.

Villa Verdi ★★
A guesthouse that's more like an oasis boutique hotel, Villa Verdi is set in lovely tree-shaded gardens, has a sparkling pool, a cosy bar and good restaurant under thatch. There are 13 standard rooms, three apartments and a luxury suite, all individually decorated. Secure parking. In Windhoek West, within walking distance of the city.
4 Villa Verdi St.
Tel: (061) 221 994.
www.leadinglodges.com

Kalahari Sands Hotel and Casino ★★★
A high-rise building dominating the skyline in the centre of town, this 173-room hotel is accessed from escalators in the Gustav Voigts shopping arcade. With bars and lounges, it has the standard 4-star facilities and offers 24-hour room service. The swimming pool is on the roof and the casino is popular. The informal

Dunes restaurant offers an à la carte menu and a buffet carvery. Convenient for shopping and walking around the city.

129 Independence Ave, Gustav Voigts Centre. Tel: (061) 280 0000. www.suninternational.com

Hotel Heinitzburg ★★★★

Deluxe rooms in a turreted castle built by Count von Schwerin for his fiancée in 1914. Its gourmet restaurant, Leo's At The Castle, has skyline views of Windhoek, and the Garden Terrace, serving meals, coffee and patisserie, is the smart place for cocktails and sunset-watching.

22 Heinitzburg St. Tel: (061) 249 597. www.heinitzburg.com

EATING OUT

Café Zoo ★★

Come here for Italian specialities in the elegant restaurant, as well as coffee and great cakes. Inside Zoo Park, with umbrella-shaded tables on a terrace beneath Windhoek's largest rubber tree.

In Zoo Park, overlooking Independence Ave. Tel: (061) 223 479. Open: 8am–10pm.

Joe's Beerhouse ★★

Popular pub restaurant with fun décor, packed with finds and memorabilia inside the restaurant and outside in the plant-packed courtyard. An atmospheric place serving big helpings of meaty German and Namibian food, as well as some vegetarian options, Joe's also has a gallery of great photography and a gift shop. Booking essential.

160 Nelson Mandela Ave, Eros. Tel: (061) 232 457. www.joesbeerhouse.com. Open: Mon–Thur 5pm– late, Fri–Sun 11am–late.

Luigi & The Fish ★★

Restaurant boasting 'the biggest menu in Namibia', which includes game, beef, pork, chicken, seafood, vegetarian and pizza.

320 Sam Nujoma Drive, Klein Windhoek. Tel: (061) 256 399. Open: noon–3pm & 6– 10pm, later at weekends. Upstairs bar open: until 1–2am.

Nice ★★★

'Nice' stands for the Namibian Institute of Culinary Education and its chefs prove how good the training is with their fusion menus. It has a selection of smart dining rooms, lounges and courtyards, a chic wine bar and a sushi bar.

2 Mozart St, corner Hosea Kutako Drive. Tel: (061) 300 710. www.nice.com.na. Open: Wed–Fri noon– 2pm, Tue–Sun 6–10pm.

Restaurant Gathemann ★★★

On the first floor of a colonial building, this airy and relaxed restaurant has ceiling fans, potted palms and a terrace overlooking busy Independence Ave. It serves stylishly presented Namibian and international dishes.

175 Independence Ave. Tel: (061) 223 853. Open: Mon–Sat noon–3pm & 6–10pm.

ENTERTAINMENT

College of the Arts

Classical music concerts, ballet and contemporary dance.

41 Fidel Castro St.
Tel: (061) 225 841.

El Cubano

Trendy bar and lounge with salsa music, food and dance.
Tal St, next to the Warehouse Theatre.
Tel: (061) 258 829.
Open: 4pm–2am.
Closed: Sun.

Funky Lab

Disco with bars, gets very crowded on weekends.
Ae Gams Shopping Centre, Sam Nujoma Dr.
Open: Wed–Sat into the early hours.

The Lounge and La Dee Das Night Club

Plays good music. Lounge upstairs, dancing downstairs.
Ferry St, Southern Industrial Area.

National Theatre of Namibia

Presents opera, ballet, concerts, drama, cabaret and children's theatre.
12 John Meinert St.
Tel: (061) 374 400.
www.ntn.org.na

Warehouse Theatre

Windhoek's favourite music scene. Events change nightly and include laid-back African sounds, classical music, vibrant kwaito, smooth and acoustic jazz, with local and international artists.
48 Tal St.
Tel: (061) 225 059.
Closed: Mon.

SPORT AND LEISURE

GocheGanas Wellness Village

Eleven treatment rooms for massages, facial, beauty and body treatments. Heated indoor pool, cave sauna, fitness gym.
GocheGanas Nature Reserve, 29km (18 miles) southeast of Windhoek.
Tel: (061) 224 909.
www.gocheganas.com

Namibia Travel Connection

Respected Windhoek-based tour operator that offers safaris or can tailor-make itineraries and arrange all travel and accommodation in Namibia.
4 Lorentz St.
Tel: (061) 246 427.
www.namibiatravel.com

Reit Safari Horse Trails

From Windhoek to Swakopmund, 400km (249 miles) on horseback. From the escarpment through the desert to the sea, adventurous 12-night riding and camping safaris for the physically fit and experienced rider.
PO Box 11778, Klein Windhoek.
Tel: (061) 250 764. www. horse-trails-namibia.com

Ster-Kinekor

Multiplex five-screen cinema showing the latest releases. Cheap on Wednesday.
Maerua Mall, Centaurus Rd. Tel: (061) 249 267.

Virgin Active

A fitness centre with aerobics, cardio circuit, weights, indoor cycling, pool, sauna, squash, toning circuit and juice bar.
Maerua Mall, Centaurus Rd. Tel: (061) 234 399.

Windhoek Golf and Country Club
Tel: (061) 205 5223.
www.wccgolf.com.na

Kalahari

ACCOMMODATION

Intu Afrika ★★★

The three lodges on the 10,000ha (24,710 acre) private Kalahari Game

Reserve are set among open grassy plains, acacia woodland and low red sand dunes. All have excellent restaurants and dinner is included in the price. Bushmen-guided walks and game drives to see Kalahari desert lions are available.

Camelthorn Lodge

Set in a secluded valley among ancient camelthorn trees, the main building is thatched and there are 11 air-conditioned chalets.

Suricate Tented Lodge

With 11 luxury tents on timber decks, the lodge is on a red sand dune overlooking pans of the Auob River, which floods in the rainy season and is home to many bird species.

Zebra Lodge

This lodge offers eight luxurious, air-conditioned twin-bedded chalets and five suites with desert views. The main lodge is relaxed and there's a secluded pool among palms.
Tel: (063) 683 218.
www.intu-afrika.com

Otjiwarongo

ACCOMMODATION

Dinosaur's Tracks ★

On the Strobel family farm Otjihaenamaparero ('Dinosaur's Tracks'), each of the three en-suite guest rooms has three beds and a patio with mountain views. There are four camping sites, shaded by trees. Payment is cash only.
Tel: (067) 290 153.
www.dinosaurstracks.com

Okonjima Lodge ★★★★

The home of the AfriCat Foundation (*see pp44–5*) consists of **Main Camp** with ten en-suite double rooms, **Bush Camp**, on the edge of a wilderness area, with eight luxury, thatched, African-style *rondavels* (bungalows), the two-bedroom, four-bed **Bush Suite** with its own private pool, kitchen, chef, guide and game-viewing vehicle, and **The Villa**, which is so big and luxurious it practically defies description.

Dinner and all activities (leopard- and cheetah-tracking, lion sightings, night visit to a hide) are included in the price. Children under the age of 12 are not accepted.

Tel: (067) 687 032
or 081 142 1195.
www.okonjima.com

Rehoboth

ACCOMMODATION

Lake Oanob Resort and Game Reserve ★–★★

Waterfront accommodation around the lake and its craggy red rock mountains. There's a thatched lake-view restaurant, bar and children's pool.

Campsites (★) come shaded, not shaded and waterfront.

Rooms (★) are single, double or family-sized. They are not self-catering and breakfast is included in the price.

Chalets (★★) have two bedrooms (max four adults and two children) or three (max six adults and two children).
Tel: (062) 522 370.
www.oanob.com.na

Waterberg Plateau Park

ACCOMMODATION

WATERBERG CAMP ★–★★★

At the foot of towering red cliffs surrounded by trees and walking trails, the camp has family-sized chalets (★★★), double rooms (★★) and a grassy campsite (★) with good ablutions. They are all some distance away from the big swimming pool and the bar/restaurant, which is housed in the old Rathaus, built in 1908, with courtyard tables under trees.

Book through Namibia Wildlife Resorts (NWR). Tel: (061) 285 7200. www.nwr.com.na

FISH RIVER CANYON AND THE SOUTHWEST
Fish River Canyon
ACCOMMODATION
Gondwana Cañon Park Cañon Roadhouse ★–★★
With an evocative Wild West feel, the Roadhouse has nine neat rooms, a good restaurant with shady terrace, a bar, pool and information centre. Also some good camping sites.

Cañon Lodge ★★
With an historic farmhouse as the main lodge, 25 stone-built chalets with thatched roofs built among massive red granite

boulders and endless desert views, this is a great place to stay within 20km (12 1/2 miles) of the Fish River Canyon. Nice relaxed restaurant with tables on the leafy terrace. Scenic flights, sundowner drives, hiking and horse riding available.

Cañon Village ★★
Accommodation is in stone-built Cape Dutch-style cottages, and the thatched main building with its restaurant and bar has murals depicting the history and culture of the Bondelswart Nama people, the early inhabitants of this area. Peaceful and pleasing, it has a 'pool with a view'.
Tel: (061) 230 066. www.gondwana-desert-collection.com

SPORT AND LEISURE
Guided hiking trails
Hiking with mules in the wilderness area around the Fish River Canyon. Campfire dinners, sleeping in tents or under the stars, for groups of 4–7 participants (children over 12), walking 15–20km (9–12 miles) for 6–8 hours a day.

Tel: (061) 264 521. www.mule-trails-namibia.com. Open: May–Sept.

Aus
ACCOMMODATION
Desert Horse Inn ★★
The main lodge at **Klein-Aus Vista** looks out on mountains and rocky desert plains and has a good restaurant with a wooden deck. There are 24 bungalow rooms, each with its terrace. **Eagle's Nest**, a 15-minute drive from the inn, has six get-away-from-it-all self-catering chalets with endless views, built into a mountain slope. Ten camping sites are also available. Hiking, 4WD game drives and sundowner visits to the wild desert horses (*see pp52–3*) are among the activity options.
Tel: (063) 258 021. www.klein-aus-vista.com

Keetmanshoop
ACCOMMODATION
Bird's Mansions Hotel ★
Comfortable hotel in town with 23 air-conditioned rooms, a courtyard beer and tea garden, heated swimming

pool with *braai* (barbecue) facilities, a good restaurant, an internet café and ample secure parking.
6th Ave.
Tel: (063) 221 711. www. birdsaccommodation.com

Bird's Nest B&B ★

This cosy house in gardens has ten air-conditioned en-suite bedrooms with television and hot-drink-making facilities, a lounge bar and secure parking.
16 Pastorie St.
Tel: (063) 222 906.

Lüderitz
ACCOMMODATION
Haus Sandrose ★

Right in town, a quiet and pretty place with attractively furnished self-catering rooms and a fully equipped flat all set around a garden courtyard.
15 Bismarck St.
Tel: (063) 202 630.

Kratzplatz ★

Friendly and comfortable B&B with a cosy breakfast room and secure parking. It's attached to Barrels restaurant (*see below*) in the area where Lüderitz began, close to Goerke House.

5 Nachtigal St.
Tel: (063) 202 458.
www.kratzplatz.com

Lüderitz Nest Hotel ★★

The best hotel in Lüderitz. Light and airy, all the 73 nicely decorated and comfortable rooms have sea views, many with a balcony. Three of the rooms have disabled access and non-smoking rooms are available. The Penguin restaurant is good, especially for fish and seafood. The Oyster Bar looks out over the ocean. The hotel has a garden pool, sauna and a children's playground.
Tel: (063) 204 000.
www.nesthotel.com

EATING OUT
Barrels ★★

One of the oldest buildings in Lüderitz, this friendly bar and restaurant serves up oxtail, goulash, steak, kässler and eisbein (pork knuckle), also cheap and cheerful sausage or pie and salad. The menu changes daily.
Berg St.
Tel: (063) 202 458.
Open: 5–9.30pm.

Ritzi's ★★

In the waterfront complex with harbour views both from inside tables and out on the umbrella-shaded deck, this is essentially an excellent seafood restaurant, but there are meat, chicken and pizza options, too.
Hafen St.
Tel: (063) 202 818.
www.ritzisrestaurant.com.
Open: 8am–10pm.
Closed: Sun.

Penguin Restaurant ★★★

In the Lüderitz Nest Hotel (*see above*). It does a good-value carvery lunch buffet on Sunday (*12.30–2pm*).
Tel: (063) 204 000.
www.nesthotel.com.
Open: light meals 10am–6.30pm, dinner 6.30–10.30pm.

SPORT AND LEISURE
Lüderitz Tours and Safaris

Lots of good local information and a selection of books on Namibia.
Bismarck St.
Tel: (063) 202 719/202 622.

NAMIB DESERT
Namib-Naukluft National Park

ACCOMMODATION

Sossus Dune Lodge ★★★★

Near Sesriem Canyon and the only accommodation within the park, which means you can reach the Sossusvlei dunes before sunrise and stay after sunset. Built from wood, thatch and canvas in an 'Afro-village' style, this top-scale lodge at the foot of a mountain has 23 well-spaced bungalows and two honeymoon suites linked by wooden walkways to the restaurant, bar and swimming pool. Dinner is included in the price.
Book through Namibia Wildlife Resorts (NWR).
Tel: (061) 285 7200.
www.nwr.com.na

NamibRand Nature Reserve

ACCOMMODATION

Le Mirage Desert Lodge and Spa ★★★★

This lodge has great character. All the 26 air-conditioned and luxurious rooms have a balcony from which to view the colours of the Namib, the restaurant is excellent, the pool tempting. A massage in the spa is heavenly. Activities include hot-air ballooning and quad biking. Dinner is included in the price.
21km (13 miles) from Sesriem.
Tel: (063) 683 020.
www.lemiragelodge.com

SPORT AND LEISURE

Desert Homestead and Horse Trails

Sunrise and sunset horse rides are the highlights of a stay at the environmentally friendly Homestead, which has 20 smart, thatched chalets and delicious alfresco dining. Sunrise riders get a treat of a breakfast in the desert, served under the shade of a camelthorn tree.
On the C19, about 32km (20 miles) southeast of Sesriem.
Tel: (063) 293 243.
www.deserthomestead-namibia.com

Namib Sky Adventure Safaris

Drifting in a hot-air balloon across a landscape of sand dunes and mountains as the sun rises is a magical, if expensive, experience. Collection from lodges around the Sossusvlei area to the take-off site, also a champagne breakfast on landing, are included in the price.
Tel: (063) 683 188.
www.namibsky.com

Sesriem

ACCOMMODATION

Sesriem Camping ★

Close to the park gate, the Sesriem campsite has been upgraded and has 24 sites, a kiosk, bar and swimming pool as well as the usual ablution blocks. Campers get entrance to the park 30 minutes before its official opening time.
Book through Namibia Wildlife Resorts (NWR).
Tel: (061) 285 7200.
www.nwr.com.na

Desert Camp ★★

Twenty luxury accommodation units, with a central bar and dining area, provide self-catering facilities for families, 4km (2½ miles) from Sossusvlei Lodge.
Tel: (063) 693 205.
www.desertcamp.com

Sossusvlei Lodge ★★★
On a 40,000ha (98,842 acre) private nature reserve, the lodge is adjacent to the Sesriem entrance gate for Sossusvlei. It has 45 rooms with adobe walls shaded, tent-like, by canvas roofs, a relaxed restaurant and pool with a view. The Adventure Centre can organise scenic flights, hot-air balloon trips, ecofriendly quad biking, and excursions to the Sossusvlei dunes. Dinner is included in the price. Non-residents are welcome for lunch (*noon–2.30pm*).
Tel: (063) 693 231.
www.sossusvleilodge.com

SWAKOPMUND AND THE COAST
Swakopmund
Accommodation
The Alternative Space ★
B&B with four non-smoking 'boutique'-style en-suite rooms, library and reading room, self-catering kitchen, communal TV lounge with an open fire, *braai* (barbecue) place and secure parking.

167 Anton Lubofski St.
Tel: (064) 402 713.
The Secret Garden Guesthouse ★
Tucked away in old Swakopmund, a short walk from the ocean promenade, this small guesthouse has six en-suite bedrooms, simply but neatly furnished, that face onto a secluded, palm-tree shaded courtyard. Facilities include secure parking, Jacuzzi, self-catering and barbecue facilities, a guests' TV lounge and licensed bar service.
36 Bismarck St.
Tel: (064) 404 037.
www.secretgarden.com.na
The Burning Shore ★★
Midway (15km/9 miles) between Swakopmund and Walvis Bay, right by the ocean, this is where Brad Pitt and Angelina Jolie famously stayed. It has laid-back, 5-star elegance, alfresco dining on the deck and smart food in the restaurant, and has a cosy fireplace in the private lounge.
152 4th St, Long Beach.
Tel: (064) 207 568. www.
africanpridehotels.com

Hansa Hotel ★★
Frequently voted 'Best Hotel in Namibia', this timeless classic, dating back to 1905, is in the heart of town, close to all the shopping and an easy walk to the seafront. Privately owned, it is elegant but relaxed, the air-conditioned rooms are spacious and very comfortable and antiques furnish the residents' lounges and library.
3 Hendrik Witbooi St.
Tel: (064) 414 200.
www.hansahotel.com.na
Hotel Schweizerhaus ★★
Family-run 2-star hotel overlooking the gardens in the centre of town and minutes from the beach. Simply furnished but comfortable en-suite rooms, most with a balcony. Disabled access.
1 Bismarck St.
Tel: (064) 400 331/2/3.
www.schweizerhaus.net
The Stiltz ★★
Nine wooden bungalows, under thatch and built on stilts, are linked by wooden walkways to the main dining bungalow at this innovative B&B. Overlooking the Atlantic Ocean, sand dunes and

the bird-rich lagoon at the Swakop River mouth, yet within walking distance of town, the bungalows are pleasingly decorated and have balconies with sand and sea views.
Strand South, past the aquarium.
Tel: (064) 400 771.
www.ctc.com.na/thestiltz

Swakopmund Hotel & Entertainment Centre ★★★
A big hotel (90 rooms) built in and around Swakopmund's old railway station (an historical monument). The air-conditioned rooms, with all the usual 4-star facilities, surround a palm-tree garden courtyard and swimming pool and are attractively decorated in modern colonial style.
2 Theo-Ben Gurirab Ave.
Tel: (064) 410 5200.
www.legacyhotels.co.za

EATING OUT

Café Anton ★
A bit of a legend in Swakopmund. Coffee, Black Forest gateau and traditional German confectionery, also light lunches, served at tables inside and on the terrace overlooking the gardens in the centre of town.
1 Bismarck St.
Tel: (064) 400 331/ 402 419.
www.schweizerhaus.net.
Open: 7am–7pm.

Lightkeeper's Cottage ★
Eat lunch on the hilltop lawn under shady umbrellas and look out to sea with the great red-and-white lighthouse beaming away behind you. Good range of salads and sandwiches, with homemade bread and some interesting fillings.
Behind the museum on the Strand. Closed: evenings & Sun.

Station Café ★
Burgers, toasts and sandwiches, steak rolls, cakes and healthy options, plus a *braai* (barbecue) on Saturdays (10am–2pm).
Otavi Bahnhof, Sam Nujoma Ave.
Tel: (064) 463 528.
Open: Mon–Fri 8am–8pm, Sat & holidays 8am–3pm.

The Blue Olive ★★
This deli with Italian flare is a tasty change from Swakopmund's mainly German-influenced menus. It serves local produce such as asparagus from the Swakop River valley, herbs, cakes and Walvis Bay oysters, has a daily special from the day's marketing and makes good olive-bread sandwiches.
6 Hendrik Witbooi St.
Tel: (064) 463 811. Open: Mon–Fri 7am–6pm, Sat & Sun 7am–4pm.

Brauhaus ★★
Busy restaurant with a range of beers and platters of traditional German cuisine plus Namibian game and fish specialities.
Nedbank Arcade.
Tel: (064) 402 214.
Open: 10am–2pm & 6–9.30pm. Closed: Sun.

Lighthouse Pub and Restaurant ★★
Great seafood with sea views in the large restaurant and a terrace ideal for sundowner drinks. Steaks, burgers and pizzas are also on the menu. Very popular, so booking is advised.
Pool Terrace, Main Beach.
Tel: (064) 400 894.
Open: 11am–10pm.

Ocean Basket ★★

Part of a southern African chain, this big and popular restaurant has some umbrella-shaded tables outside. It serves up large portions of inexpensive fish dishes from fish and chips to combos (try the kingklip and prawns) and seafood platters.

The Mole, beneath the Strand Hotel.
Tel: (064) 401 102.
www.oceanbasket.com.
Open: Mon–Sat 11am–10pm, Sun 11am–9pm.

Platform One ★★★

Smart, Victorian-themed restaurant in the Swakopmund Hotel & Entertainment Centre. À la carte menu and speciality buffets for dinner. Also open for 'finger lunch' platters. The Station Grill, in the same complex, is known for fresh fish and steaks.
2 Theo-Ben Gurirab Ave.
Tel: (064) 410 5200.
Open: noon–2pm & 6.30–10pm.

The Tug ★★★

An old tugboat provides the setting for some memorable seafood and ocean views. With nautical décor, the bar has portholes and the dining area is built around the ship, with tables out on the deck for warm evenings and lunch (weekends only). Booking essential.
Strand St, by the jetty.
Tel: (064) 402 356.
Open: Mon–Fri 5–10pm, Sat & Sun noon–3pm & 5–10pm.

Zur Kupferpfanne ★★★

Namibian and German cuisine in a 1902 building with antique furniture and almost a museum of memorabilia.
Corner Daniel Tjongarero Ave & Tobias Hainyeko St. Tel: (064) 405 405.
Open: 6–10pm.
Closed: Sun.

ENTERTAINMENT

Atlanta Cinema

Attractive little cinema showing new releases. Small café in the foyer.
Brauhaus Arcade.
Tel: (064) 402 743.

Mermaid Casino

Poker, roulette and slots.
Swakopmund Hotel & Entertainment Centre, 2 Theo-Ben Gurirab Ave.
Tel: (064) 410 5200.
Open: 10am–late.

SPORT AND LEISURE

Alter Action

Lie-down or stand-up sand boarding on the 'perfect' dune – a 100m (330ft) star dune with six different faces. Full instruction and safety equipment are provided. People of every age are welcome. Children aged ten and up are usually confident on their own boards, and younger children can ride with guides on the faster descents. Snowboards with soft boots and bindings are used for stand-up boarding.
Tel: (064) 404 737.
www.alter-action.info

Camel Farm

Camel rides in the desert.
12km (7 miles) east of Swakopmund, well signposted off the B2 Swakop-Windhoek road.
Tel: (064) 400 363.
Open: 2–5pm.

Dare Devil Adventures

Quad biking (automatic and semi-automatic bikes) and dune-boarding. There's a supervised kids' track for while you're away in the dunes.

Opposite Long Beach between Swakopmund & Walvis Bay.
Tel: 081 128 4492/ 129 0010/127 6005.

Desert Explorers Quad Biking Tours

Guided quad bike groups are led through the Swakop River mouth into the dune belt to ride the roller-coasters, berms, spirals and slopes of high dunes. Automatic, semi-automatic and manual bikes are available for tours lasting between 45 minutes and two hours. The company also offers sand boarding (both lie-down and stand-up), horse riding, tandem skydiving and paragliding.
Desert Explorers Adventure Centre, on the left side of the Swakop River Bridge.
Tel: (064) 406 096.

Desert Paragliding Club

Introductory courses and flights with instructors qualified to train from novice to expert levels. Tandem flights also available.
62 Nathaniel Maxuilili St.
Tel: (064) 463 371. www.
desertparagliding.com

Hata Angu Cultural Tours

Lie-down and stand-up sand boarding. Full safety gear and instruction from experienced sand boarders.
Tel: (064) 461 118.
www.
culturalactivities.in.na

Living Desert Tours

Run by naturalist Tommy Collard, a half-day adventure through the dunes in a 4WD vehicle to find the 'hidden' creatures of the desert, including the gecko, sidewinder adder, 'sand-diving' lizard, chameleon and burrowing skink. He also does 'Living Desert' night walks and trips to remote Sandwich Harbour.
Tel: (064) 461 038.
www.tommys.iway.na

Namib-i

Information centre for Swakopmund and the surrounding Erongo region. Maps, reservations, activities and tour bookings.
Corner Sam Nujoma Ave & Hendrik Witbooi St.
Tel: (064) 403 129/ 404 827. www.namibi.org

Rossmund Golf Course
Tel: (064) 405 644.
www.swakopresorts.com

Scenic Air

Scenic flights in light aircraft to destinations including the Skeleton Coast, Sossusvlei, Brandberg mountain, a Himba village in Opuwo, Lüderitz and the Fish River Canyon.
Sam Nujoma Ave.
Tel: (064) 403 575.
www.Scenic-Air.com

Swakop Tour Company

Off-the-beaten-track guided nature drives, for individual travellers and small groups of four people, in the company of desert-aficionado George Erb. Explores the fauna, flora and fascinating aspects of desert ecology and geology.
Tel: (064) 404 088 or 081 124 2906 (all hours).

Turnstone Tours

Full-day guided excursions in custom-built 4WD vehicles to remote Sandwich Harbour. Transfers from/to your accommodation and lunch are included.
Tel: (064) 403 123.
www.turnstone-tours.com

Cape Cross

ACCOMMODATION

Cape Cross Lodge ★★

A short distance from the seal colony (but well out of the 'smell zone'), this lodge is a stylish find on the isolated Skeleton Coast 120km (75 miles) north of Swakopmund. It has 30 large airy rooms, all with a sea view from their balconies, though the eight rooms at the front are the stars of the show, with their panoramic sea vistas. Sitting on the deck and watching seals play in the ocean close by is a pretty good reason to spend a day or two here. Others are the cool décor of soft blue and white furnishings, the excellent restaurant (open to non-residents for lunch only, noon–2pm) and well-stocked, if quirky, wine cellar. Dinner is included in the price.
Tel: (064) 694 012.
www.capecross.org

Walvis Bay

ACCOMMODATION

Esplanade Park Cottages ★

Good-value municipal self-catering accommodation, 27 one- and two-bedroom bungalows, set on shaded lawns overlooking the lagoon.
The Esplanade. Book through Walvis Bay Resorts.
Tel: (064) 215 500.
www.wbresorts.com.na

Lagoon Lodge ★★

Painted cheerful yellow, this guesthouse opposite the lagoon has eight rooms, all with views of the water, and a small pool in the garden at the back. Endless birdwatching opportunities.
2 Kovamba Dr.
Tel: (064) 200 850.
www.lagoonlodge.com.na

Protea Hotel Pelican Bay ★★★

Very modern and stylish hotel with 50 air-conditioned rooms, one with disabled access, at the edge of the lagoon. Smart restaurant, bar and a 24-hour coffee shop. Plenty of pelicans to entertain you.
The Esplanade.
Tel: (064) 214 000.
www.proteahotels.com

EATING OUT

Harry Peppar ★★

The pizza parlour that gets rave reviews.
Corner 11th Rd & Nangola Mbumba Ave.
Tel: (064) 203 131.
Open: 11am–late.

The Raft ★★★

Built on stilts in the lagoon and reached by a long boardwalk, this innovative restaurant serves seafood, steak, pasta and salads and you get a great view of pelican fly-pasts. The bar is good for sunset watching, too.
The Esplanade.
Tel: (064) 204 877.
Open: noon–3pm & 6–10pm. Closed: Sun (low season).

SPORT AND LEISURE

Catamaran Charters

The 13m (46ft) catamaran sails into the lagoon for sightings of seals, dolphins, white pelicans and possibly leatherback turtles and surfacing whales. Oysters and savoury snacks are served on board.
12th Rd, Walvis Bay, next to Probst Bakery.
Tel: (064) 200 798. www. namibiancharters.com

Dune Lover Tours

Self-drive guided excursion to Sandwich Harbour in an open-air Yamaha 4WD. Includes dune and beach driving, explanations of desert life, bird and wildlife sightings.
Lagoon Lodge, Nangolo Mbumba Drive.
Tel: (064) 200 850.

Dune 7

Sand boarding on the highest dune in the coastal dune belt, about 10km (6 miles) outside Walvis Bay. The dune is 130m (426ft) high with a very steep slip face of soft, powder-like sand. Quad bikes are used to shuttle boarders to the top of the dune. Professional instruction is given.
Tel: (064) 220 881 or 081 127 7636.
www.duneseven.com

Eco Marine Kayak Tours

Using single and double kayaks, Jeanne Meintjies takes visitors onto the lagoon for two-hour birdwatching trips among flamingos and pelicans. No previous kayaking experience is necessary and the boats are stable and easy to steer on the calm water. Longer trips are also available to the seal colonies at Pelican Point.
Tel: (064) 203 144.
www.emkayak.iway.na

Levo Tours

Seal and dolphin cruises by ski-boat through Walvis Bay harbour to Pelican Point. Pelicans, flamingos and cormorants are among the seabirds seen in abundance. Friendly seals come on board the boats to be fed, while dolphins swim around nearby. Oysters, champagne and snacks are served at the seal colony. Trips with this well-established company, which also operates beach or boat fishing trips, are one of the most popular coastal excursions.
Tanker Jetty, 14th Rd.
Tel: (064) 200 709.
www.levotours.com

Mola Mola

Ski-boat marine cruises to see the birdlife, dolphins and seals, with oysters and snacks on board. 'Marine Dune' days combine a morning on the water with the afternoon spent in the desert on a 4WD excursion to Sandwich Harbour.
Booking office, Atlantic St, The Esplanade.
Tel: (064) 205 511.
www.mola-namibia.com

DAMARALAND
Northern Damaraland
ACCOMMODATION
Gelbingen Guest Farm ★★

The Himba settlement on this farm attracts many day visitors, but you can also stay in one of the four guest chalets. Meals (Namibian home cooking) are served in the shady *lapa* (thatched outdoor eating area) with its bar, there's a swimming pool and game drives are offered. Trophy hunting, too. Dinner, bed and breakfast are included in the rates.
Kamanjab.
Tel: (067) 330 277.

Grootberg Lodge ★★★

Perched at the top of the Grootberg Pass, this place affords phenomenal views down the wide Klip River Valley from the main lodge building and the 11 delightful stone-and-thatch cottages on the

rim of the plateau. This is a friendly and relaxed venue, with superb food (dinner is included in the rates) and fine attention to detail. It has a horizon pool, and game drives, walks, horse riding and visits to a conservancy village are all available, but unless you have a 4WD and a steady nerve, don't attempt the drive up to the lodge. Park at the (guarded) site on the road and someone will come down to collect you. A great find, and one of Namibia's special places.
On the C40, 90km (56 miles) from Kamanjab.
Tel: (061) 246 788.
www.grootberg-lodge.com
Palmwag Lodge ★★★
Thatched bungalows and luxury en-suite tents are shaded by tall makalani palm trees near a tributary of the Uniab River. The restaurant overlooks hills, there are two swimming pools, and game drives take you in search of black rhino, desert elephant, springbok, kudu and giraffe. There are walking trails, and visits to a

Himba village are also possible. Dinner is included in the price. A few self-catering camping sites (★) are also available.
Tel: (064) 404 459.
www.palmwag.com.na

Southern Damaraland
ACCOMMODATION
Aba-Huab Community Campsite ★
Sites equipped with fireplaces, tables, benches and running water are scattered along the (usually dry) Aba-Huab riverbed. There are four ablution blocks with hot showers and flush toilets. This award-winning campsite, with a fully licensed bar and restaurant, can accommodate up to 120 guests. Tents with bedding, thatched A-frame shelters and rooms are available for rent.
On the D3214, 6km (4 miles) from Twyfelfontein.
Tel: (067) 331 104.
www.nacobta.com.na
Twyfelfontein Country Lodge ★★★
The extensive use of thatch, plus natural stone

and earthy paint colours, means the ecofriendly lodge buildings blend into the red rock cliffs that tower above them. The lodge is on the Uibasen Twyfelfontein Conservancy and stays here contribute income to local communities. There are even original San (Bushmen) engravings on the rocks at the entrance. Meals are big buffets, with the dinner carvery offering up to ten roasts. The price includes dinner.
Central Reservations.
Tel: (061) 374 750.
www.namibialodges.com

ETOSHA NATIONAL PARK
Inside the park
ACCOMMODATION
Halali ★★
The 'middle' rest camp, less used and generally quieter than the others, Halali has a stylishly designed restaurant with outside terrace tables, and accommodation that ranges from honeymoon suites with outdoor Jacuzzi to self-catering family bush chalets and elegant rooms. The

floodlit waterhole is set slightly away from the accommodation, among boulders and shady mopane trees.

Okaukuejo ★★

The biggest of the three rest camps in the park, Okaukuejo has everything from stunning thatched *rondavel* chalets by the huge floodlit waterhole to elegant rooms and camping facilities. A big swimming pool, restaurant, bar, shops, an internet centre and post office are all on site.

Namutoni ★★★

The most stylish and spectacular of the three rest camps within the park, Namutoni has stunning rooms and two very good restaurants in the old German Fort, which has been cleverly renovated to give an atmospheric setting. The swimming pool is shaded by tall makalani palms and the waterhole has a thatched seating area. Dinner is included in the price. Camping sites are also available.

Book all three through Namibia Wildlife Resorts (NWR).
Tel: (061) 285 7200.
www.nwr.com.na

Bordering the park

ACCOMMODATION

Eagle Tented Lodge and Spa ★★★

In the Epacha Private Game Reserve, which has 21 species of antelope and black rhino. Luxuriously huge safari tents, each with its own splash pool, are set on raised wooden decks with panoramic views over the everlasting bush. The main lodge is stone and thatch, has a relaxing lounge and an excellent restaurant. Treatment rooms in its Mystique Spa even look out to the horizon, as does the pool. Dinner is included in the price.
Tel: (067) 687 161.
www.eagletentedlodge.com

Epacha Game Lodge and Spa ★★★★

Set in the 21,000ha (51,892 acre) Epacha Private Game Reserve, Namibia's first 5-star lodge is large and luxurious with 18 extremely spacious air-conditioned chalets, all individually decorated and furnished with antiques, scattered across the hillside. The main lodge has a stylish restaurant, bars and lounges, infinity pool and the pampering Mystique Spa. Dinner is included in the price.
Tel: (067) 697 047.
www.epacha.com

CAPRIVI STRIP

ACCOMMODATION

N//goabaca Community Campsite ★

Run by Kxoe Bushmen, a small campsite with views of the Popa Falls. Flush toilets, hot showers, water taps. Suitable for well equipped 4WD visitors with their own food and supplies.
East of the Divundu bridge. Tel: (061) 255 977.
www.nacobta.com.na

Mahangu Safari Lodge ★★

Near the Mahango National Park and West Caprivi Park, this thatched lodge has seven bungalows and four big en-suite safari tents, all with air-conditioning, plus good camping sites with power points. There's a dining, bar and lounge area, a pool with river views and two sunset decks on the riverfront. Activities include game and bird viewing by boat, tigerfish and bream fishing and game drives in the nearby Parks.

PO Box 5200, Divundu. Tel: (066) 259 037. www.mahangu.com.na

Ndhovu Safari Lodge ★★★

Luxury en-suite tented accommodation on the western bank of the Okavango River and overlooking the Bwabwata National Park. The thatched lounge/dining area overlooks the river, where elephants and hippo sometimes congregate. Over 400 species of birds have been recorded in the area. Sundowner cruises, fishing excursions, village tours and game drives are offered. The price includes dinner. The Lodge also has a camping site.

PO Box 5035, Divundu. Tel: (066) 259 901. www.ndhovu.com

Divava Okavango Lodge & Spa ★★★★

Twenty luxurious air-conditioned chalets are set in established gardens, each with an outside shower and a private balcony with vistas over woods and water. The main building overlooks the Okavango River and has an impressive viewing deck, swimming pool, restaurant, bar and wine cellar. Nature walks, boat trips to see hippos and crocodiles, tigerfish angling and visits to Caprivian craftspeople are available. The price includes dinner.

Divundu, near the Popa Falls. Tel: (066) 259 005. www.divava.com

BUSHMANLAND

ACCOMMODATION

Nhoma Camp

Small wilderness camp with six twin safari tents near the Bushman village of //Nhoq'ma, 80km (50 miles) from Tsumkwe. The price includes all meals and guided activities with the local community.

PO Box 1899, Tsumeb. Tel: (081) 273 4606. www.tsumkwel.iway.na

Nyae Nyae Conservancy

Encounters with Ju/'hoansi Bushmen to experience their hunter-gatherer skills and traditional way of life. Basic but well-cared-for campsites.

Nyae Nyae Tsumkwe. Tel: (067) 244 011. Or in Windhoek through NACOBTA, tel: (061) 255 977. www.nacobta.com.na

SKELETON COAST FLY-IN SAFARIS

SPORT AND LEISURE

Skeleton Coast Safaris

Organises small group ecotourism excursions by light aircraft and 4WD vehicles between three tented camps in the northern reaches of the remote Skeleton Coast.

Shop no 15B, 2nd Floor North Wing, Maerua Park, Windhoek. Tel: (061) 224 248. www. skeletoncoastsafaris.com

Wilderness Safaris

Fly-in safaris to the Skeleton Coast National Park staying in the company's own eco-friendly and very comfortable camp that can accommodate a maximum of 12 people.

PO Box 6850, Windhoek. Tel: (061) 274 500. www.wilderness-safaris.com

Index

Acknowledgements

The author wishes to thank Louise Ellison at Namibia Travel Connection for her invaluable help in organising the lengthy research trip around Namibia for the preparation of this guide.

Also members of the Leading Lodges of Africa – Villa Verdi Guesthouse, Intu Afrika, Le Mirage Desert Lodge & Spa and Eagle Tented Camp & Spa – Cañon Lodge and Klein Aus Vista of the Gondwana Collection, Twyfelfontein Country Lodge, Grootberg Lodge and Okonjima Bush Camp for their hospitality and assistance. And Johan Kotze for his patience and impeccable driving.

Thomas Cook wishes to thank the author, Sue Dobson, for the loan of the photographs reproduced in this book, to whom the copyright in the photographs belongs (except the following).

DREAMSTIME N Smit 17; A Rayson 26, 147; F Doctor 27; J Richards 48, 125; Möller 68; Hkratky 77, 90; Piccaya 96; D Sabo 124; D Lacroix 130; Schoeman 131
PICTURE COLOUR LIBRARY R de la Harpe 57, 89; L Poelders 60
FRANÇOIS POOLMAN 15
WORLD PICTURES/PHOTOSHOT 106, 119

For CAMBRIDGE PUBLISHING MANAGEMENT LTD:
Project editor: Diane Teillol
Copy editor: Anne McGregor
Typesetter: Paul Queripel
Proofreader: Jan McCann
Indexer: Marie Lorimar

SEND YOUR THOUGHTS TO
BOOKS@THOMASCOOK.COM

We're committed to providing the very best up-to-date information in our travel guides and constantly strive to make them as useful as they can be. You can help us to improve future editions by letting us have your feedback. If you've made a wonderful discovery on your travels that we don't already feature, if you'd like to inform us about recent changes to anything that we do include, or if you simply want to let us know your thoughts about this guidebook and how we can make it even better – we'd love to hear from you.

Send us ideas, discoveries and recommendations today and then look out for your valuable input in the next edition of this title.

Emails to the above address, or letters to Travellers Series Editor, Thomas Cook Publishing, PO Box 227, Unit 9, Coningsby Road, Peterborough PE3 8SB, UK.

Please don't forget to let us know which title your feedback refers to!